TEACHING ENGLISH IN
PRIMARY CLASSROOMS

TEACHING ENGLISH IN PRIMARY CLASSROOMS

*Mina Drever, Susan Moule
and Keith Peterson*

Trentham Books

First published in 1999 by Trentham Books Limited

Trentham Books Limited
Westview House
734 London Road
Oakhill
Stoke on Trent
Staffordshire
England ST4 5NP

British Cataloguing in Publication Data
A catalogue record for this book is available from the
British Library
ISBN 1 85856 177 9
(hb ISBN 1 85856 178 7)

Cover picture: Drawing a Shelter – a perfect example of pupils
collaborating in planning and executing a task.

Designed and typeset by Trentham Print Design Ltd., Chester and printed in
Great Britain by Cromwell Press Ltd., Wiltshire.

Contents

AKNOWLEDGMENTS

Teaching English in Primary Schools is the result of many people's co-operation. In our thanks we would like to single out the children in our classrooms, whose enthusiasm for learning to manipulate language enabled us to enjoy exploring with these new ways of teaching it. Our headteachers – Mr Ian Gibson at Parkgate JM School in Watford and Mr Terry Jukes at Fleetville JM School in St Albans – gave us unrelenting support, both through our training programme in 1996-1997 and throughout the process of translating our lessons into this book. We would also like to thank Hertfordshire MECSS (Minority Ethnic Curriculum Support Service) for providing the training and in particular Shahla Taheri-White and Jan Hardy for giving us their blessings in writing this book. Equally supportive was Keith C. Dawes at the DfEE (Department for Education and Employment) who gave us permission to mention the GEST (Grants for Education Support and Training) training programme during which all this new language teaching took place.

Several original texts were used in our classroom lessons, either in their original format or adapted. These texts, and the task sheets derived from them, have been reproduced in this book exactly as they were used in the lessons. We are grateful to the following publishers for granting us permission for this reproduction: Scott Dunn World for The Best of Tanzania; Basil Blackwell Limited for the list of pronouns from A Dictionary of Linguistics and Phonetics by David Crystal; Pearson Education Limited for grammatical examples from A Student's Grammar of the English Language by S. Greenbaum and R. Quirk, and from A Communicative Grammar of English by J. Svartvik; The Orion Publishing Group Ltd for the story The Librarian and the Robbers from Great Piratical Rumbustification by Margaret Mahy; Scholastics Children's Books for the poem Eddie in Bed, from Quick Let's Get Out of Here by Michael Rosen and Quentin Blake.

Every effort has been made to trace copyright holders whose work appears in this book. Any errors or omissions, which may be brought to our attention will be rectified in future impressions.

We would also like to thank those who read earlier extracts of this book, in particular Gillian Klein and her team of editors. And a special thanks to John Stipling for his hard work and his technological skills in producing the book. Any mistakes and omissions are solely our responsibility.

Mina Drever

PREFACE

If you are reading this book the chances are that you are involved in teaching English in primary school. Whatever your role, you are obviously interested in finding out how other class teachers are tackling a subject which has been, and continues to be, in the political and educational spotlight. Our attitude to teaching English has changed considerably in the last few years, not least due to the pressures of raising standards across the educational spectrum. This enlightenment may have come about with the increasing realisation that all learning relies heavily on having a good grasp of the workings of English.

English across the curriculum is not a new notion of course. But how English is used in different subject areas is not something we may have dwelt upon, for example, that scientific English uses a great many passive expressions. Are all primary children aware of this? Should they be? What about words that we assume children, and adults come to that, really understand just because we use them every day? You will find that the word stage gives Keith Peterson's class a headache!

All teachers want the children in their charge to achieve the best possible standards and therefore they will do all they can to assist them in this aim. But how does one go about teaching how language works? We have gone through a generation or two thinking that we don't need to learn the language we are born to acquire because we do it so brilliantly from birth. If we are young bilingual learners, we have been told not to worry about that either, because we acquire a second language quite painlessly. The fact that we already possess the gift of our first language will assist us in learning a second or third.

Such theoretical positions came as a relief to those of us who hated teaching grammar, steeped as it was in the stale, you-are-not-meant-to-enjoy-this approach to the study of language. This is where this book is a breath of fresh air. The study of language can be as interesting, exhilarating, stimulating and fun (FUN?) as a teacher wants to make it.

Susan Moule and Keith Peterson are two such teachers. Their enthusiasm for the study of language is infectious. Their classes have fun exploring the words we use in the English of history, of geography, of poetry, of the media – and how these words are put together to create accurate and appropriate meanings. So the study of subject specific language and the investigation of the grammar of that language (see how Susan's class takes apart the verbs in a poem) takes on a new dimension which is in keeping with the requirements of the National Curriculum and of the Literacy Hour.

INTRODUCTION

The strategies in this book for teaching English in primary classrooms were originally designed for primary class teachers to teach English to bilingual pupils. They were subsequently, and successfully, adopted by the same teachers to teach English to all the children in their classes: that is children whose first language is English and bilingual children. By bilingual is meant children who may speak even more than two languages. Indeed, some of them may speak English, a home or first language, and they may be literate (that is they may read but not speak it) in a third language. For example many Muslim children learn to read classic Arabic in order to learn to read the Quran, but do not speak any other versions of Arabic, like Syrian or Egyptian Arabic.

In 1995 the Department for Education (DfE – which in 1996 became the Department for Education and Employment – DfEE) set up a programme of GEST (Grants for Education and Training) to education authorities who were successful in their bids to receive this grant. The essential criterion was that authorities should provide training to class-teachers (in primary schools, subject teachers in secondary schools and classroom assistants in both) on how to teach English to bilingual pupils. The programme ran for three years. Each of the years had a GEST number. GEST 16 – 1995/96 (DfE);. GEST 11 – 1996/97 (DfEE);. GEST 7 – 1997/98 (DfEE).

The GEST 11 remit to local authorities trainers was:

> To equip mainstream, class and subject teachers and classroom assistants, through in-service training, with the skills needed to respond to linguistic diversity in the classroom, and promote pupils' mastery of English thus securing full access to the National Curriculum (DfEE, circular 9/95 – Grants for Education and Training 1996/97).

Generally, the Language Services sections of each educational directorate were responsible for bidding for this grant and, upon success, implementing the above directive. The work presented in this book represents part of a comprehensive training programme, which I designed for the client schools of MECSS (Minority Ethnic Curriculum Support Service) in Hertfordshire in my capacity as GEST 11 Adviser for primary schools. The function of these Language Services is to provide specialist language teaching in schools with bilingual pupils on roll.

The training programme in Hertfordshire drew on teachers' own needs. It was important not to impose impractical ideas, which the teachers themselves could not implement. The training I had in mind would do two things: a) fulfil the DfEE remit, and b) encourage teachers to buy into a systematic training scheme based on research findings which indicated the most effective strategies to teach English in the classroom.

A Needs Analysis with class-teachers and head-teachers in MECSS client schools revealed two teacher needs:

- Class-teachers wanted to know what to teach, when and how, to bilingual pupils and it all had to fit in the National Curriculum requirements

- Whatever strategies I suggested had to be incorporated in the teaching of the whole class.

The implications from these two points are enormous and, it will be seen, are well integrated in the programmes of teaching strategies adopted and employed by the two teachers in this book, Susan Moule and Keith Peterson.

What to teach when?

First of all, why did the teachers want to know what to teach when to bilingual pupils? Their rationale was that there must be a sequential process to language development. It makes logical sense. And if there is a sequential process to language development, this must suggest that certain aspects of language should be taught before others.

Indeed the Language Acquisition research literature has convincingly demonstrated that there is a sequential pattern in which we acquire our first and subsequent languages. Studies of young children acquiring English as a first language have examined how children develop their knowledge and use of specific areas of English, for instance the acquisition of morphemes, the development of negation and question formation, vocabulary and verb systems. The first area of language development to be observed in very young children was morphology. Countless studies have been repeated which supported the original findings that there is a strict order in which children acquire certain morphemes. For example children learn to use base verbs in the present continuous (daddy reading) long before the appropriate form of the auxiliary verb to be to express the same idea (daddy is reading). In morphological terms this is translated as: the morpheme –ing is acquired before the auxiliary be, which, incidentally, is acquired after the morpheme singular –s of third person singular in regular verbs.

The term morph is a Greek word meaning form. In linguistics morphology is the study of the form of words. Morphemes are the smallest units in words. Morphemes can be single words, which have their own meaningful sense, like is of the verb to be: these are called free morphemes. Or morphemes can be a small part of a word: for example the ed of the regular past tense changes the form of a verb to which it is added to change its meaning (brake+d): these are called bound morphemes. The interesting phenomenon that was discovered about morphemes – because they attracted a lot of attention from linguists – is that when we learn English as a second language, we apparently acquire these morphemes in a sequential order. Though the ordered sequence does not mirror exactly the order of first language acquisition, certain morphemes are learned before others. And this appears to be true for all learners of English as a second language, regardless of which first language they speak, Chinese or Spanish, Hindi or French.

There is order, therefore, in how we learn English as a first and second language. To make it clearer, let us look briefly at the development of negation:

Development of negation in English as a first language – EL1	Development of negation in English as a second language – EL2
Stage 1 the child utters simple two/three word sentences beginning, or ending, with no, e.g. *no milk* – which can mean a variety of things, including *I don't want any milk, there's no milk* etcetera; adults understand children from the context these little phrases are uttered in. **Stage 2** the beginning of a more complex use of sentences, which contain more adult-like grammar, though still with errors e.g. *he don't want it.* **Stage 3** children begin to use auxiliary and modal verbs correctly e.g. *I don't want it*	**Stage 1** a classic negative utterance from a learner of EL2 is something like *I no like it,* mirroring the EL1 child who puts *no* in front of what is being negated. **Stage 2** starting to use *don't* without subject agreement, e.g. *I don't want it, he don't want it* **Stage 3** other auxiliary and modal verbs begin to be used in the negative e.g. *I can't go.* **Stage 4** the use of *do* in negation becomes correct e.g. *he doesn't like it.*

These stages have been taken from Patsy M. Lightbown and Nina Spada, 1996, How languages are learned. This is a good, quick read on the acquisition of both first and second language.

These and numerous other findings on language development (for a detailed account on language development see Jean Berko Gleason, 1997, The development of language) would suggest that the teaching of language in the classroom should follow this spontaneous ordering of grammatical rules. It would be safe to assume that there are conceptual and cognitive reasons why this is so. For example, it makes sense that the acquisition of morphemes shows that the regular plural – that is words which are pluralised by simply adding the morpheme s – is acquired by young children before they acquire the irregular plurals, eg. women. If we think about it, regular patterns may be easier to notice than irregular patterns in our physical environment. In the linguistic environment regular grammatical rules are probably learned before exceptions to these rules purely because they are easier to recognise.

This way of thinking guided the design of the strategies presented in this book. Susan Moule and Keith Peterson take a developmental approach to teaching a verb tense:

• identify the verb

• define the role of the verb in the sentence

• understand the concept of time as expressed by the verb

• introduce the appropriate metalinguistic terminology

• select the categories of verbs on which to focus.

How to teach the *what*

This is the most difficult concept to translate into practice in the classroom. The **how** is not merely a set of activities and tasks which may be interesting, appealing, pertinent and fun. It isn't a method or a technique or an approach. It is all these things and more. **How** is the **way** in which we present a linguistic puzzle to the pupils in the classroom:

• the words we choose with which to present the puzzle

• the sequences we select in presenting it

• the materials we design

• the use we make of the materials

• the learning behaviour we want the children to adopt in different activities

• the roles we play as teachers

• the roles we want the pupils to enact in the learning process

• the timing of all these.

The most pertinent issue in the context of teaching English in a primary classroom in which pupils come from diverse linguistic backgrounds is that the class-teacher has to consider the linguistic needs of all the children in the class. There is no time to give one-to-one tuition on a continuous basis, desirable though this may be. We have seen that language acquisition moves more or less along equivalent lines of development in EL1 and EL2. Of course, the actual proficiency of the bilingual children in the class will be at different levels. But so is the proficiency of speakers of English as a first language. It is therefore crucial to develop strategies, which will encompass all of these variables to the maximum linguistic benefit of all the children. The strategies presented in this book have been developed by analysing the research literature of studies carried out in the instructional context to see which are the most effective to the development of language, both first and second language.

All-inclusive strategies

The second point made by the Hertfordshire teachers during the Needs Analysis was that the strategies had to incorporate the whole class. They expressed two basic concerns:

- A class teacher cannot devise two lessons, one for bilingual children and one for English speakers. How can lessons take care of all the individual dif-ferences in the classroom? With greater emphasis on whole-class teaching, this is impossible. Whilst it is imperative that differentiation be a key factor, what the teachers wanted was a way of teaching English to the whole class before differentiated group or individual tasks could be drawn from the whole-class activities.

- The class teachers I talked to expressed a strong feeling that what was good enough for the bilingual children had to be good enough for the mono-lingual English-speaking children whose competence in the English language – so the teachers said – was way below the standard required for academic study.

At the end of the Hertfordshire training programme 90% of the teachers who had participated were unanimous in their evaluation-questionnaire that the strategies were effective in the English language development of all the children in their classes. The strategies were not subjected to any experiment but these teachers could see evidence of their efficacy among the pupils.

Let us think a little more about linguistic diversity in the classroom. Assume that your classroom's profile reads something like this:

fifteen children speak English as a first language (EL1)

five children speak Urdu – they are learners of English as a second language (EL2)

one child speaks Chinese – who is also an EL2 learner

one child speaks Italian – for whom English may be a third language.

These children speak between them four national languages. That is, the lan-guage of a large linguistic community which comes under the large umbrella of either 'English', or 'Chinese', or 'Italian'. But is this really the case? How many varieties of English are spoken in England? Which one of the many hundreds of languages spoken in China does your Chinese child speak? The Italian child in your class would certainly understand two of the hundreds of different languages spoken in Italy – let's say Sicilian and Italian. These are discrete languages. Many 'Italian dialects' have their grammar and bilingual dictionaries (D'Ascoli, 1993; Valente, 1982). However the 'Italian' child in your class will be literate in only one of these two languages. Doubtless it would be Italian because that is the official linguistic code of the whole of Italy, which includes Sicily. So all the children in your class will speak either different 'varieties' of the language that is attributed to them, e.g. a local 'dialect', like Cockney English, Liverpudlian English, Mancunian English by the English children. For an enjoyable read on this aspect of languages and dialects try A Mouthful of Air by Anthony Burgess.

The language of the larger community – let us call it the official language – is one linguistic code known by the members of that community. The language spoken by the groups within that community may be a different linguistic code, more localised and shared by the members of the smaller social group. Now, this concept may be alien in England. The localised 'varieties' of English are considered inferior, a sad state of affairs. But in other countries, such as in the Arabic-speaking world and in Italy, 'dialects' are not considered inferior languages. In the Middle East, China, Italy and so on, children grow up quite naturally switching between the official dialect and the local dialect. (I use the term dialect to refer to a group of languages, which belong to a family of languages. For example French, Italian, Spanish, Portuguese, Romanian belong to the family of Romance dialects.) In schools these children are taught the official dialect of the wider community, which is the language of academic education. In essence, they are taught as bilinguals who know two languages: one they speak, but are not literate in, the local dialect, and the official code in which they need to attain a high level of competence in order to achieve high standards in their academic studies and, consequently, in the world of work.

It may be academically useful to think of your fifteen children who speak English as a first language as bilinguals. How many EL1 children say things like 'He don't want it' like the EL2 learners at stage two of acquiring the English system of negation on page 3? What about such utterances as 'ain't it?', 'it's gonna be', 'he were hiding'? They're fine in their appropriate context. It is a linguistic speaking code, which must not be stamped upon. But your fifteen EL1 children will not see these phrases written down in historical accounts, or a geography text, or a mathematical equation. Indeed, do these EL1 children know that it's gonna be is a future tense which translates as it's going to be in Standard English dialect? See how Keith Peterson teaches the future tense (chapter 3) to his whole class, as if all the children were bilinguals.

This book, therefore, promises to place its approach to teaching English in wider perspectives than hitherto.

- All the children in the class – whatever spoken dialectical code they bring to school – are taught to approach their learning of English as a different linguistic code which will enable them to communicate with wider audiences, including inanimate audiences like school books

- We place our teaching firmly in research findings on the best way to assist language development in the classroom: what strategies have been tested in experimental conditions? Many teachers have good practices. However, good practices may not be transferable unless all the variables have been carefully considered. The advantage of experimental investigations is that the conditions are generally well defined. It is therefore easier to assess whether one approach to teaching would have any chances of succeeding in a different context

- Our central aim is to teach children to reflect on the use of language and especially on the way words (ALL words) are manipulated to create intentional meanings. There will be no understanding between the creators and receivers of meanings (YOU and ME; WRITER and READER) unless all participants to the discourse share the same understanding of the linguistic code used in the production of the meaning.

There are five chapters:

Chapter 1: A rationale, based on research findings, is presented, in order to explain why we teach language the way we do.

Chapter 2: English teaching and learning at Parkgate school in two Year 4 classes. Children learn to collaborate on a writing project in one class while a different class discovers that meanings expressed by verbs can vary depending both on the forms (present versus past tenses) of the verbs and on their semantic relations: what images do they conjure up in the reader of a poem?

Chapter 3: A different school – Fleetville JM – and two Year 5 classes. One class focuses on the meaning of collaboration and how it assists us in shaping our thought processes. These thoughts are constructed to fulfil a number of criteria. They must make sense to our partners. Therefore they must encompass the objectives set for learning. They must be expressed with appropriate vocabulary and sentence structure to fit the task The other class discovers that language, like mathematics and science, geography and history, has its own metalanguage, i.e. terms with which to describe language. They learn to define their own use of the future in terms of its positive and negative aspects. These are important transferable cognitive skills.

Chapter 4: Two more lessons here, on how to teach two sticky grammatical points: the possessive's – to a Year 4 class – and relative pronouns, to a Year 6 class. The approach is simple: start with what children are familiar with and extract the grammar from it. Central to learning is the children's participation in the learning. This sounds like stating the obvious: but we all know that children can develop a detachment to the task, which becomes mechanical. They don't always know what they're doing.

Chapter 5: A short concluding collection of thoughts and observations tie it all together.

CHAPTER 1
THEORETICAL FRAMEWORK

Mina Drever

The English language teaching strategies presented in this book have been designed within the theoretical frameworks of collaborative learning and of explicit grammar teaching. Each contributes to the development of language in the primary classroom. All the children in our primary classroom are developing competence in more than one linguistic code. The strategies designed and applied in this book aim to promote proficiency in the linguistic code which the National Curriculum calls Standard English. This dialect will be learned by children who may speak a local or regional variety of British English and by children who may speak, and be literate in, languages quite dissimilar to English, for example Panjabi. This book will use the term English language to refer to this Standard English code.

In chapters 2, 3 and 4 the programmes for teaching various aspects of the English language have been constructed on the evidence of research findings that these strategies do positively promote the development of linguistic proficiency. Investigations into language acquisition, language learning and language development generally divide themselves into studies of first language (L1) and studies of second language (L2). So our teaching approaches have drawn on findings in both areas of linguistic interest. It is beyond the scope of this book to give in-depth and detailed analysis of these studies. We can only refer to major findings, but these indicate the direction of the empirical research and, consequently, the way we may need to conceptualise teaching language in the classroom. But first:

WHAT are: collaborative learning and explicit grammar teaching?

WHY have we adopted these approaches?

HOW do they work in practice?

1

COLLABORATIVE LEARNING

WHAT IS IT?

Collaborative learning is one of several approaches, which centre on group learning with varying degrees of differences between them. For example, the nature and organisation of the working groups, the quality and quantity of teacher involvement and the degree of explicitness in teachers' instructions will identify a particular collaborative learning style as: 'Student Team Learning, Learning Together, ... Group Investigation, ... the Structural Approach, ... Complex Instruction, ... and the Collaborative Approach' (Davidson, 1994, p.13). Others will talk of Co-operative Learning (Murray, 1994). But they all have certain common characteristics, namely:

- a common goal for the group

- shared resources

- individual accountability to the group

- mutual interdependence between the members of the group

- reflective thinking.

These features appear on the surface to be straightforward. In all our teaching we have clear aims and objectives. When we set groups to work we instruct them on what to do by modelling and giving exemplars. We ask children to work together, help one another, and share. We empower children by giving them opportunities to organise themselves, to be investigative and to explore their own learning. However there are certain aspects of our normal way of doing things which we worry about, if we are honest. For example, do some children always dominate? do lower ability children tend to shy away from taking leading roles? does group work often break down? do some children take an inordinate amount of time to complete a task? Some never finish?

In fact teachers are often frightened of upsetting lower ability children, of embarassing and humiliating them and so don't single them out in oral tasks, for example. When teachers brave themselves to face this challenge, they tend to: '...ask them questions that require lower level cognitive responses and give them less time to respond and fewer hints than they give pupils for whom they have higher expectations' (Murray, 1994 p.4).

What does collaborative learning offer to assist teachers and learners to avoid these pitfalls? Let us look at two aspects of the child's development: the social and the cognitive.

From the social point of view pupils will experience in a collaborative group learning situation: debate, argument, negotiation, a sense of equal partnership, a sense of belonging, distribution of labour according to pre-set and fair criteria, high expectations, mutual motivation, collective success, mutual respect, peer support (Biott and Easen, 1994; Haworth, 1992; Pagett, 1992; Murray, 1994; Udvari-Solner, 1994).

Children who are given these experiences will do no more than imitate the processes of their normal social relationships on which the development of human mental functions depends (Vygotsky, 1934). Vygotsky sees children's conceptual development as dependent on the common perspectives of the community in which they are growing. The community intervenes in and contributes to the children's social (and cognitive) adaptation by providing instructional support, without which they would not be able to go beyond the level they're at in order to reach their 'zone of ... proximal development' (p.187). This in no way implies that children have no ability to develop concepts by themselves via the power of their own reasoning. On the contrary, the community, and collaborative learning in the classroom, work with the children's inner resources to accelerate their socialisation and concept development (Vygotsky, 1934).

In a sense, if used properly, collaborative learning is an excellent tool for moving children away from their egocentric view of the world (Piaget, 1959), i.e. when children see themselves as the centre of the universe and their own perspective is the one that matters. In collaborative learning they have to learn to listen to others' opinions, consider them with due respect, accept that there may be different, and sometimes better, routes to solutions.

This process of socialisation contributes to cognitive growth. 'The ability to perform in novel situations is the hallmark of human cognition' (Anderson, 1982 p.391). One process involved in cognitive development is sorting out conflict, not necessarily in a negative sense. Conflict can be a positive learning experience: recognising that there may not be, sometimes, a right and wrong solution but a compromise. The socio-cognitive aspect of conflict is the process by which a 'learner is confronted with other conflicting views' (Biott and Easen, 1994). Therefore '..collaboration might be seen as a 'deconstructive' learning process in the sense that it is likely to demand a challenging of existing ideas and a questioning of taken-for-granted assumptions' (p.188).

There have been, and continue to be, conflicting views on the development of, and interplay between, language and cognition. On the one hand language and cognition are seen as separate unitary constructs (Cromer, 1976, 1988; Gopnik and Meltzoff 1986). On the other hand intelligence is considered to be multi-dimensional and language but one function of cognition (Gardner, 1983). Language learning is a cognitive function dependent on the development of skills also required in other areas of cognition (Ellman, 1990), such as encoding information, processing it, decoding it, storing it either in short term, for immediate use, or long term memory for later retrieval. All of these learning skills will be honed in a collaborative learning situation in which problem solving – 'a fundamental category of cognition' (Anderson, 1982 p372) – features prominently.

WHY HAVE WE ADOPTED COLLABORATIVE LEARNING?

What have all the above arguments got to do with language development? Why do we think that collaborative learning will assist language learning?

Language is a social situation in which 'learners construct meaning collaboratively' (Haworth, 1992 p.43). In the course of task-based conversations Haworth discovered that only one group out of four was successful – in terms of how its members operated in the group and in terms of the group's goal achievement – in two classes in Years 6 and 7. This group was able to bring reciprocal skills to its negotiations of meaning and be reflective about its members' contributions to the discussion. Reflection involves abstracting oneself from the normal use of language and focus on how the content is being conveyed (Pratt et Grieve, 1984) for major impact on its targeted audience. It is 'the ability to think about thinking' (Haworth, 1992 p.42).

In chapter 2 of this book Susan Moule applied collaborative learning to a writing project because she wanted her class to appreciate that writing, in the real world, is often not a solitary event. In fact, collaborative writing is a 'literary event' in which 'the text is constructed through oral discussion' (Murray, 1992 p.101) in order to find 'areas of shared understanding' (p.103). It involves 'social and interactional rules' (p.102) without which it is not possible to produce successful collaborative writing. The participants of a 'literary event' bring with them disparate sets of experiences which will influence the interpretation of a text which is the focus of discussion, and the conception of the text to be written by the group. Negotiation of how these experiences will influence the intended outcome is essential, as it is in bridging the 'information gap' (p.101). The information gap arises from the differential linguistic, as well as subject-specific, knowledge, which will bear on the collaborators' interpretation of both the model text and the text to be written. Linguistic forms do affect how meaning is both conveyed by the writer and understood by its readers. Reciprocal exchange of ideas, opinions, comments and advice, choice and feedback is an essential requisite to oral planning of a piece of collaborative writing. Besides getting the obvious group dynamics right (see below, in the HOW part of this section) successful collaborative writing depends also on no-text-ownership – i.e. no individual has produced the model text, which is the 'source of new information and new language' (p.107). This could create conflict of interest and appropriation.

Negotiation of meaning is integral to using language appropriately in the execution of tasks set in our classrooms in this book. The outcome may stray considerably from the goals set. Keith Peterson (chapter 3, lesson 7) found that during a group activity in his collaborative learning project none of the children had understood what he had meant by 'doing things in stages'. He had explained to the class that their task was to design the building of a shelter in four stages, taking into their considerations the materials they had selected for the construction, the climate and the terrain of the location. All the home-groups went to their work stations, seemingly unperturbed by any aspect of the task. As Keith went around monitoring the work in progress and eavesdropping on the groups' conversations, he realised that he and his pupils had a different idea of the meaning of stage in this context. See the transcript of the video-recorded whole-class discussion – in lesson 7 – for elucidation on how Keith and his class negotiated and arrived at the correct meaning of this particular, context-bound meaning of the word stage. Similarly Susan Moule's class (chapter 2 – collaborative learning and verbs, lesson 3) seems to have no conception that the verb 'to feel' has anything to do with the tactile sense of touching. See Susan's evaluation of this at the end of the grammar work on verbs.

Misunderstanding interlocutions can be due also to minimal linguistic elements not traditionally thought of as grammar, such as yeah, mm hm and mm (Gardner 1998). Each of these minimal responses by a listener can have different meanings – and consequently affect the course of the conversation – according to the intonation with which they are expressed. Mm hm can mean 'please continue' with a falling-rising intonation, or merely an acknowledgement with a rise-fall contour. Yeah with a falling intonation indicates understanding and/or agreement, but wishes the previous speaker to pick up the conversation with a fall-rising contour. Mm with a falling intonation indicates that the listener wishes to change the conversation topic, while a fall-rising contour, like yeah, wishes to pass the reins of the discussion back to the previous speaker (Gardner, 1998). These responses are feedback to the speaker and can have a bearing on how the conversation continues. In a linguistically diverse classroom they may cause considerable confusion in sorting out the intentions of the speaker who utters them. Second language learners of English may not use these conversational items with the same frequency as native speakers and it is debatable whether they pick them up effortlessly and without intervention and appropriate feedback (Gardner, 1998).

Language use is a co-ordination of comprehension and production skills. Yet comprehensible output is not always what language learners produce, especially learners of a second language (Cummins and Swain 1986). Their performance in the second language

> ...is limited in two ways. First, the students are simply not given – especially in later grades – adequate opportunities to use the target language in the classroom context. Secondly, they are not being 'pushed' in their output. That is to say, the immersion students have developed, in the early grades, strategies for getting their meaning across which are adequate for the situation they find themselves in. There appears to be little social or cognitive pressure to produce language that reflects more appropriately or precisely their intended meaning: there is no push to be more comprehensible than

they already are. That is, there is no push for them to analyse further the grammar of the target language because their current output appears to succeed in conveying their intended message (p.133).

One of the problems with producing comprehensible output, say Cummins and Swain, is that second language learners do not always receive appropriate correction by their teachers to modify their linguistic behaviour. Teachers are often reluctant to highlight weaknesses in their lower ability pupils for fear of upsetting them. This attitude may extend towards bilingual learners, by talking more to advanced speakers of the second language (Owen, 1996). However, children do not have such reticence. Primary school age children do provide negative feedback to their non-native counterparts (Oliver, 1995). What's more, they respond 'differentially to the grammaticality or ambiguity' of their bilingual peers. They will ask for clarification ('hm?', 'what?' p.474-477) when errors occur with use of pronouns, word order, wrong use of auxiliary words, omission of other words, omission of subjects of verbs. Children will correct errors of plurality and subject agreement by responding with an utterance which includes the correct form of the error.

Feedback is not a strategy that we have concentrated on in this book. It is an important teaching strategy which requires another book to give the justification and attention it deserves because there is a great deal of controversy surrounding it. It is mentioned here, in passing, because collaborative learning is discussion-driven. As such, the differential responses by a listener will affect the 'continuous flux' (Gardner, 1998 p.209) of the conversation between members of the collaborative group. And this must be a positive influence on the development of language as it is used in negotiations of meaning, which may require a great deal of linguistic and paralinguistic attention, adjustment and manipulation, depending on the verbal and contextual cues which speakers pass around. Speakers, on receiving feedback from the listeners, may decide to change what they may have been about to say purely on the basis of signals they receive – says Gardner,

> In addition, recipients monitor the talk they are hearing not only for their emerging meanings, but also for possible points at which speakership transfer can legitimately occur, i.e. points at which a current speaker can become a listener, and a current listener can become a speaker. Roles are also continually changing as part of this flux. This implies an on-going monitoring of the relevant features of the context by all parties engaged in talk (p.209).

HOW DOES COLLABORATIVE LEARNING WORK?

Collaboration works best: if it makes thinking explicit, if thinking involves reflection, if it provides opportunities to verbalise thoughts and reflection, if 'distribution of power' is conducive to the above three points. (Biott and Easen, 1994 p.196)

> Collaboration would seem to support learning best if it makes thinking explicit. Having to put ideas into words when talking, rather like writing, can enable reflection on one's mental processes. Unlike writing, talking to oneself tends to be regarded as a rather peculiar habit. Working with others provides a ready-made audience and, potentially, introduces the need to articulate ideas and explain one's thinking. Even so, whether this will happen or not may depend upon another condition – participants' perceptions of the distribution of power and its use within the collaboration (p.196).

This has implications for:

- group organisation and group dynamics

- group's goal

- learning activities

- teacher's role

- timing.

Group organisation

- Heterogeny
  '... groups should be heterogeneous across ability levels, ethnicity, gender, and socioeconomic level. More perspective taking, elaborative thinking, and exchange of information have been noted as beneficial outcomes of heterogenous counterparts' (Udvari-Solner, 1994)

- Cohesion
  In a cohesive group '... there is no sense of individual ownership of ideas; each evaluation is made openly and co-operatively, indicating equal roles within the group ..[and] a willingness to alternate major and minor roles within the discussion' (Haworth, 1992 p.46)

- Size
  Groups should be small in numbers – 5 to 6 maximum; bigger groups break down the necessary interactional skills required in collaborative interactions, including those of feedback and choice (Donaldson, 1994; Murray, 1994).

- Selection
  The most successful groups – in terms of achieving their common goal – were those selected by the teacher on the basis of the last three criteria. Both Haworth (1992) and Biott and Easen (1994) found that self-selected groups

did not always work well together. In self-selection children will automatically form friendship groups. The problem with these is obvious: exclusion of non-friends, leading to feelings of rejection and isolation. On the other hand, teacher selected groups

'worked surprisingly well together....Even at an early stage of the project, as they tried to get to grips with their particular part of the problem, they were also exploring what it means to work together and maintain a common focus. In doing so, they were learning what was really involved in belonging to a group and contributing to its endeavours' (Biott and Easen, 1994 p.173).

Friendships are pretty precarious, especially at primary school level. Here today, gone tomorrow! When it comes to learning, it may well be advisable to match skills to the tasks involved rather than to personalities. This is where the teacher's role has to be subtle and delicate, and quite firm too. More about this below.

• Roles
  First of all there has to be individual accountability by all the members of the group (Biott and Easen, 1994; Davidson, 1994; Murray 1994; Udvari-Solner, 1994)

  Secondly, there has to be positive interdependence – the group's success to has be seen as greater than individual achievement (Davidson, 1994; Haworth, 1992; Murray, 1994).

We have seen with selection of the groups that the teacher-selected combinations are more successful than self-appointed friendship groups. The extra ingredient for an achieving group is role allocation by the teacher in such a way that the roles are interdependent (Udvari-Solner, 1994). These roles may vary according to the task, but may include:

• reader

• writer

• illustrator

• reporter

• 'jargon-buster, materials manager, quality controller' (p.64) among many.

• the group will need a chairperson or leader or facilitator – the label varies but it implies one role i.e.

  – making sure that all members interact and contribute equally

  – intervene to suggest solutions based on the preceding discussion

  – keep the discussion focused

  – prevent going off-target.

A warning by Biott and Easen: 'some children who appeared to be leaders were merely bossy' (p.47).

Group's goal

A collaborative group will need to have a prescribed academic goal (eg. make a list) and be clear about the skills which its members will need to apply to the task to achieve that goal (Udvari-Solner, 1994).

In brief the group's goal consists of:

- a shared outcome – towards which all members contribute equally

- clear objectives – staging posts towards the goal

- team study and practice – observation, discussion, drafting

- processing of skills – eg. selection of materials, investigation, fact-finding

- imitating the academic behaviour of all members of the group

- motivating each other towards the goal.

Learning activities

Davidson (1994) has identified 5 phases of learning in the collaborative approach:

- engagement
  the teacher presents the perspective of the learning task to the whole class and gives the basis for the ensuing group activities

- exploration
  the students engage in initial exploration in small 'home groups'

- transformation
  home groups reshape and transform the information given – they organise, clarify, elaborate and practice

- presentation
  by home groups of their findings to the whole class

- reflection
  look back at what they have learnt and at the process of learning which they've just experienced.

Reading Keith Peterson's collaborative learning project will show you how this format is strictly adhered to. Reflection could be the most important aspect of collaborative learning. This rarely takes place in the classroom. Routine group work normally ends at the presentation stage. Yet reflection will also enable pupils to formulate questions as well as answers as pupils are taught to be brutally inquisitive in their quest for answers by their classmates about their own progress in the project.

Teacher's role

The following list of what the teacher should do to organise, orchestrate and manage a collaborative learning situation is attributed to Biott and Easen (1994, p.206-209). However all the literature mentioned on collaborative learning in this chapter does make varying references to some if not all these aspects of collaborative learning:

- Train the class to work collaboratively

- Make expectations clear to the whole class

- Teach pupils to be responsive to how others learn best

- Enable, and constrain, the group's shared understanding of the processes involved

- Organise a range of paired and group activities

- Ensure that there is no supremacy displayed by any member of the group

- Intervene to avoid dominance in the group

- Monitor the learning of the group; listen without being obtrusive

- Display own uncertainty and invite children to offer solutions which could be useful to other learning groups or/and to the whole class

- Conduct systematic enquiry and review throughout the lesson.

Time

Apparently research indicates that:

> while 75% of the day was allocated for academic instruction, only 25% of the day was actually spent in engaged learning time, that is, students interacting with materials or actively responding (McNeil, 1994 p.243).

Harper et al (1994) found that, next to clarity of teacher instructions and practice, time spent by students thinking about, and working on, instructional content 'directly' affects 'academic achievement' (p.231). So the length and the quality of the learners' involvement in a task will influence not only the outcome of the task but also the learning inherent in the task. Teachers can exert a degree of control over three types of time, which, if used properly, add instructional value to the learning:

> Allocated time: amount of time scheduled for a particular task

Engaged time: time during which the learners are actually engaged with an academic task

Academic learning time: the amount of time during which the learners are successfully engaged in instructional pursuits which lead to a learned outcome.

These principles are employed in the collaborative learning projects presented in chapters two and three in this book. It will be interesting to read what happens in both teachers' classes when the rules, of group organisation and timing, are relaxed a little. Basically cohesion is lost, power play begins to rear its ugly head and the groups become confused to the point of individuals' distress. Collaborative learning, therefore, is a powerful teaching and learning approach which benefits children's developing cognitive and linguistic skills – but only if it is well managed by both teachers and learners.

EXPLICIT GRAMMAR TEACHING

WHAT IS IT?

To answer this question we need to break it down. First of all I will try to define grammar as it is conceptualised in the lessons in this book. Secondly, the concept of explicitness will be discussed vis–a-vis the teaching of grammar in the classroom. Both these notions, however cannot be considered without the users of the grammar and the receivers of explicit instruction, i.e. the learners in the classroom. So, a third issue to think about is language learning: what is it exactly?

A definition of grammar

There are four 'grammar' lessons in this book. Two are on the verb, one on the possessive s and one on relative pronouns. We will call these grammatical elements syntactic structures. Syntax is the way words are put together to construct complete sentences which make sense. Syntax is one component of the grammar of language. Three other components are phonology (the study of the sound system of language), morphology (the study of the forms of language) and semantics (the study of the meaning in language). Phonology, morphology and semantics are closely intertwined. For example, the –ed of the regular simple past tense, (in the lesson which focuses on this tense, see chapter 2), is a bound morpheme (see definition in the introduction, p.3). When added to a free morpheme – eg. walk – it makes up a new word, with a new meaning – walked – and a new pronunciation. Phonological rules inform us on the pronunciation of walked, and the possessive s. However, in our lessons we focused on syntax, and in particular on how the three syntactic structures introduced above – the verb, the relative pronoun and the possessive s – are constructed in meaningful sentences.

Our approach to teaching grammar can be summarised as follows:

- It is meaning based –
  We try to bring to the children's attention that words like verbs can be, and are, manipulated by speakers and writers:

  - to give expression to the way one sees the world

  - to interact with other individuals or groups of people or a readership

  - to create spoken or written text in order to construct the other two

  (Halliday, 1975)

- It is functional
  Words are used to construct sentences in order to create messages, which 'are, successively, generated, encoded, transmitted, decoded, and interpreted' (Sebeok, 1994 p.106).

- It is a cognitive process
  The study of grammatical forms requires a degree of metalinguistic awareness, which is 'the ability to reflect upon and manipulate the structural features of spoken language' (Pratt and Bowey, 1984 p.129).

These theoretical frameworks which have informed our grammar teaching are firmly interlocked. We believe that the use of language emerges out of many mental operations and physiological structures of the brain which work together, like the instruments of an orchestra, to produce vocal, and written, communication (Deacon, 1997).

Let's start with the message:

> A message is a sign or a string of signs transmitted from a sign producer, or source, to a sign receiver, or destination. Any source or destination is a living entity or the product of a living entity, such as a computer, a robot, automata, or a postulated supernatural being... (Sebeok, 1994 p.6).

The message has to be meaningful; it has to make sense to the receiver. Both the generator and the receiver of the message must share a set of rules which underlies the linguistic system which has produced the message. The linguistic system encompasses the semantic system (meaning making), the phonological system (vocalisation of meaning) and the structural system (sentence construction). The latter is the tool with which we turn meanings into vocalisations (Halliday, 1975). This is the adult system. When children attain this threshold they will have developed metalinguistic awareness, the ability to:

> abstract themselves from the normal use of language and focus their attention upon the properties of language used to convey content rather than the content itself (Pratt and Grieve, 1984 p.129).

Children are aiming for the adults' heightened sense of what language is and how it is constructed. The adult language awareness has developed in three stages:

- from the unconscious automatic control of language

- to the actual awareness of some of the forms of language, i.e. the ability to abstract the linguistic forms from the content

- to conscious awareness, i.e. explicit and intentional manipulation of linguistic units
  (Titone, 1993)

Titone differentiates between language awareness, metalinguistic awareness and metalinguistic consciousness:

Language awareness – is implicit, unanalysed knowledge of language and its functions; it is spontaneous but unreflective; it is intuitive; it recognises forms and patterns by holistic perception; it is a maturational outcome.

Metalinguistic awareness – is the ability to think and reflect upon the nature and function of language; it includes word awareness (Bowey and Tunmer, 1984), phonological awareness (Nesdale, Herriman and Turner, 1984); syntactic awareness (Tunmer and Grieve, 1984) and pragmatic awareness (Pratt and Neasdale, 1984).

Metalinguistic consciousness – the 'formal, abstract explicit knowledge of language features and functions of language as a sign system' (Titone, 1993 p.84); it implies explicit cognition; deliberate control and choice; it is reflective; it analyses formal elements.

So our approach to the teaching of grammar is holistic. It incorporates:

- raising children's awareness at the word level, which can be conceived as a symbolic sign, (Deacon 1997). This will enable them to develop referential competence. For example, the ability to think of a verb as a means to create a poetic climate (chapter 2), as well as a lexical word, which can be transformed to express temporal events and aspects at the sentence level (chapters 2 and 3).

- the study of grammatical features in their own right which involves learning appropriate metalanguage, i.e. the correct terms for labelling, defining and explaining grammatical structures. The children in our classes learn to define verbs and to identify nouns and subjects as referents of relative pronouns. The aim is for the children to develop metalinguistic consciousness in Titone's terms, so that children may be able to answer such questions as 'How do you know such an event has already taken place?' with something like 'because the verb is in the past tense'.

Both these approaches involve teaching children to reflect on the language they use and the language they hear and read, so that they may learn to make informed linguistic choices in their own productions, because

> ... reflective thinking transforms confusion, ambiguity and discrepancy into illumination, definitiveness and consistency (Dewey, 1958 p.67).

This way of conceptualising grammar suggests a system of symbols with which the human mind can execute two procedures in the aural/oral modalities:

* comprehend vocalisations uttered by other people

* produce vocalisations for other people to comprehend

and, in the written modality:

* to comprehend graphically constructed representations of thought processes by other writers

* produce graphically constructed representations of own thoughts for other readers to comprehend.

Comprehension will depend on a heightened sense of:

* metalinguistic awareness in order to make appropriate acceptability judgements on whether a sentence is well-formed or not

* and metalinguistic consciousness in order to appreciate why a sentence is not well-formed at the theoretical level of grammar and have the meta-linguistic knowledge to put it right.

Explicit instruction

In our definition of grammar we have implied that an explicit knowledge of the linguistic system is the goal of grammatical instruction in this book. From the literature on language teaching and learning it is possible to derive a scale of explicitness illustrated in the following list. Starting from the most explicit at the top to the least explicit at number 7 are some approaches whose referenced study can be looked at in greater detail in the HOW part of this section on explicit grammar teaching.

In this book instruction is unambiguous and it encompasses all the varying degrees of explicitness. It will be clear from the grammar lessons described in it that we

* focus on form as well as on forms. The grammar structures are contextualised within the sphere of children's experiences of the world and cognitive development. We look at the structures themselves, and how they are used in communicative interactions, be these oral or written or both.

- we check that the input has been processed by the children by asking them questions which elicit in the answer the targeted grammatical forms. For example 'What did you do in the playground at break today?' (chapter 2) elicits such responses as 'We played football': the focus form is the regular past tense.

- we analyse the forms in terms of:

  - the structural constituents which make them up (eg. base verb + auxiliary to express the future aspect, chapter 3)

  - the ideational and interpersonal functions for which they are used (Halliday, 1975, 1994). (For example, in chapter 4 of this book, on relative pronouns).

Type of explicit instruction	General characteristics
1. Explicit grammar teaching with clear step-by-step procedures and instructions (Doughty, 1991).	1. Teaching grammatical structure; practice, training sessions; learners left in no doubt that they are learning rules and told how to apply them.
2. Focus on forms (Spada and Lightbown, 1993).	2. Drawing learners' attention to the forms of grammatical structure in a very specific way but in communicative and interactive tasks.
3. Functional analytical (Harley, 1989).	3. Learners encounter a targeted grammatical feature in a number of different activities so that their use can be analysed and learned contextually.
4. Grammatical tasks (Fotos, 1993).	4. Learners are given tasks which contain a targeted structure and then they are tested in such a way that their answers reveal whether they have noticed these forms in the tasks.
5. Input processing (De Keyser, 1997).	5. Basically a task of comprehension; first learners encounter a grammatical rule which is explained to them in general terms; a text is read or heard and then understanding is tested by asking questions in such a way that the targeted grammatical rule must be used in the answer.
6. Enhanced input (Robinson, 1997).	6. For example, highlighting grammatical forms visually so that learners notice them.
7. Focus on form (Spada and Lightbown, 1993).	7. Analysis of how grammatical forms are used in a variety of curricular areas.

- we enhance the input in written grammatical tasks using a variety of texts in order to draw children's attention to particular targeted words as they are used in different phrases, sentences, texts.

- we are explicit in

  - our use of grammatical terminology

  - instructions pertaining to grammatical terms

  - the grammatical knowledge which we expect the children to have learnt in a particular lesson or series of lessons.

We are convinced that explicit instruction has to include all these approaches. It is doubtful whether on its own enhanced input would succeed in achieving long term retention of learning. It may be a good strategy to start with, as we do with our lesson on the future aspect of the verb (chapter 3). If we had left our work on the future there, with a text containing words which had been highlighted, boxed or underlined, I wonder how many of the children would have noticed (Fotos, 1993; De Keyser, 1997) and how many would have understood it? None, certainly, would have been able to discuss it in metalinguistic terms, as they eventually learn to do, employing all the approaches in the table above.

The sequence of these approaches is almost immaterial. The children's chronological age and cognitive stage will suggest an appropriate starting point. Generally we do this by combining

- text
- children's chronological age
- children's cognitive stage
- children's experiences of the world, which include both personal and academic life.

We are making two assumptions in our approach to grammar teaching:

- explicit instruction leads to implicit and explicit learning by the child
- it is desirable for children to aquire explicit grammatical knowledge

These assumptions will be discussed below, in the WHY part of this section. We will conclude this discussion on the nature of explicit grammar teaching by considering briefly what language learning entails.

Language learning

There is no absolute consensus – in applied linguistics, psycholinguistics or cognitive psychology – on how language is learned. There are a number of theoretical perspectives, some of which are at extreme points of the argument.

This is a huge field of knowledge and it seems insulting to gloss over it as we must in this chapter. However, a few allusions to the research literature will place our own thinking in the bigger picture. For more informative reading on language acquisition and development, the following publications are recommended, with full references in the bibliography: Language Development, edited by Jean Berko Gleason; The Handbook of Child Language, edited by Paul Fletcher and Brian MacWhinney; Input and Interaction in Language Acquisition, edited by Claire Gallaway and Brian Richards; The Study of Second Language Acquisition, by Rod Ellis.

Over the last forty years there have been some strong arguments between the nativists and the non-nativists. Basically nativism posits a biological foundation for language, founded on linguistic theory (Chomsky, 1957, 1965). This means that the brain is hardwired before birth to acquire language. The evidence for this has been sought in the manifestly rapid way very young children – from age 18 months approximately – pick up the language of their environment, be it English, or Mandarin or Swahili. What's more, there is a universal pattern in this effortless acquisition:

- It is sequential – i.e. some linguistic forms are acquired before others (Brown and Bellugi, 1964; Brown 1973)

- It is maturational – i.e. in tandem with chronological age; by 24 months, for example, children are constructing two word utterances and by age 4 all the basic grammatical structures are in place, even if children make production errors along the way.

- It does not always mirror adult grammar. Children will utter phrases they've never heard adults say and appear not to produce as much more salient items in adult speech. For example irregular verbs (eg. sleep/slept; break/broke) appear more frequently in adult speech than regular verbs. Yet, when children are beginning to construct their own sentences, they attach the regular past tense formation (eg. shopped) to irregular verbs as well as regular ones. They construct such words as comed instead of came. What is interesting about this is that children generally begin to use irregular verbs correctly at first and, for some inexplicable reason, then start over-generalising the application of the regular –ed version.

- Nobody teaches this language to children (Gold, 1967). Children acquire language in this way all over the world. How can this be? There has to be in the brain a structure that is responsible for language learning, a sort of language acquisition device, a LAD (McNeill, 1966, 1971). This device enables children to construct the linguistic system of the environment they are born in. In essence LAD has blueprints for any grammar of any language to be learnt. When children encounter a particular grammar, LAD searches its templates, on behalf of the children, and looks for patterns that match this particular grammar. Thus it enables children to grow up learning to speak English in some parts of the world, while other children may be working out how Japanese, Somali or Eskimo are constructed (Chomsky, 1957,1965).

These theories developed in the sixties, and were followed by numerous observational studies in many different linguistic environments in the seventies and eighties. This way of conceptualising language acquisition is very appealing. It sounds almost magical. Parents and grandparents who hear children's command of language develop if not by the hour then by the day, marvel at this wondrous gift of language.

Few people dared raise their voices publicly against such powerful thinking in order to challenge it in open court, as it were (Braine, 1971, 1994; Hebb et al, 1971; Honey, 1997; Howe, 1993; Sampson, 1997; Staats, 1971). But a great deal of empirical investigation was taking place during these years, both in the field of second language acquisition and cognitive psychology. The sceptics among applied linguists and experimental psychologists were looking at, respectively, the effects of instructional input to language development, and language learning in the sphere of general learning mechanisms. A chronological illustration (opposite) of these different theoretical approaches may give a clearer picture of where we've come from and where we are at now vis-à-vis language learning.

This illustration indicates that language was considered a learnable skill up to the early sixties. It became an acquisitional phenomenon in the seventies and eighties. In the nineties it is one of many learnable cognitive skills. In reality there are grey areas between all of these theoretical approaches (Bohannon III and Bonvillian, 1997). In each approach there is the implication that there are two basic types of learning: the implicit and the explicit. Both depend on the interaction between environmental variables and the human brain's predisposition to learn language (Deacon, 1997; Greenfield, 1997). For example, imitation in the behaviourist sense is a conditioned process, which leads to learning via reinforcement, repetition, and a reward system. From a linguistics perspective it is a process of unconscious learning via exposure and observation. Interactionists, on the other hand, make use of disguised elicited imitation by priming children and providing them with a variety of informative feedback (Bohannon III and Bonvillian, 1997). For example, parents, and other adults interacting with children, may recast or/and expand their children's incorrect utterances. In this way adults inform children that there is something wrong with what they've just said. For example, if a child says: 'My foots hurt', the adult may say: 'Your feet hurt'. In the case of an expansion children's incorrect words are corrected and expanded by the adult. For example, a child may say: 'Milk gone', and the adult may say something like: 'Yes, you're right, the milk has all gone'.

In essence, what is changing, is not the question of how language is acquired or learned, but the way of asking the question. Now we know more about the brain's physical structure. There is no LAD. There is no one single area of the brain that is responsible for language but several regions which contribute to the function of language (Deacon 1997; Greenfield 1997). With what we know about the brain, we can ask different types of questions pertaining to language learning.

Period	Theoretical approach	Characteristics
>>>>>>> 1960	Behaviourism	Language is a habit formation achieved by: • repetition • reward • practice • conditioning
1960s	Cognitive Constructivism And Linguistic Theory	Children construct the grammar of their language with the help of LAD • linguistic theory • language universals • universal grammar (UG)
1970s >>>>>1980s	Nativism	Supports UG and LAD • Acquisition is central • Learning is peripheral
1990s	Experimental Psychology And Cognitive Psychology	Interactionism: i.e. all areas of cognition and psychological development interact in the process of language learning: • practice effects • connectionism • implicit learning • explicit learning

For example, if we accept that 'language learning is the learning and analysis of sequences' (Ellis, 1997 p.45) – eg. sound sequences in words, word sequences in phrases and sentences – we would be viewing language as a problem-solving activity. Accordingly we would want to know how the brain goes about identifying sequences, sorting them out and recalling them. Sequential conceptualisation does not pertain only to the realm of language learning: neither do categorisation and classification of sequences. So it would make sense to question whether the thinking process involved in these procedures is a cognitive skill which, once learned in one domain, can be applied in other areas of learning. These problem-solving procedures may involve a thinking process of Adapted Control of Thought (ACT) (Anderson, 1982) which, once learned in one area of cognition, can be transferred, adapted and applied to a different sphere of learning.

ACT proposes that cognitive skills are acquired in two stages: the declarative stage and the procedural stage.

*   declarative stage – the brain receives new information or a new set of facts; the brain stores these facts in its working memory, sometimes called short-term memory; the working memory rehearses these facts, juggles them about and builds up propositions about them based on previously learned knowledge which is now stored in the long-term memory

*   procedural stage – the brain runs through a set of procedures in order to produce a solution to the problem, by: retrieving data from long-tem memory of previously learned knowledge; looking for sets of patterns/ rules/forms which matches the new information; selecting the one/s that match the newly received information.

The thinking may go something like this:

Here is a new problem

I need to find a way of solving it

Somewhere in my memory bank there must be a way of doing it

Let me see: is there something I already know which looks like/sounds like this new problem or any aspect of the problem?

If so, all I have to do is find the match.

Let us look at a linguistic example and how ACT would solve it. If the linguistic problem is to put the word man in the plural, the mind will search for rules on pluralisation. What the mind already knows about the rules of English pluralisation will tell it that:

*   if the word is a countable noun and it is regular, then add an s to make it plural – this is the general rule of English plurality

- if the word is a countable noun and it is irregular, find the appropriate plural form – this is the specific rule of English plurality, i.e. the specific is the exception to the rule.

The formula for this problem-solving procedure is: IF >>>>>>then, IF not >>>then.

For example:

– if the goal is to generate the plural of a regular count noun, then use the regular rule of English pluralisation and add an s.

– if the goal is not to generate the plural of a regular count noun, then find the specific rule for this particular count noun.

This problem-solving procedure is based on a hierarchy of goals and subgoals in which selection and production are sequential and serial. That is, a general rule is selected and applied before a specific one is selected and applied. It sounds like a very long and twisted path and it is difficult to imagine the mind taking so long in solving such a small problem as putting a small word into the plural. Think of the mistakes children make in primary schools. Maybe it is not such an insignificant linguistic problem after all. ACT (Anderson, 1982) proposes that the more a rule is applied successfully, the stronger becomes the specific knowledge and the faster its application. By the 'power law of practice' (p.397), the more frequent the practice, the less time is taken to find the solution. With practice we get to 'knowledge compilation' (p.383) which allows for two or more sequences of production to be collapsed into one 'composition' (p.383). Composition is the procedure whereby data from long-term memory is called into the working memory and held there only long enough for the problem to be solved, and then sent back. The procedural stage, therefore, becomes automatic once the specific rule is applied before the general rule is retrieved because it is not needed.

If we were to consider this general theory of learning, then our approach to language teaching in the classroom may become more like problem solving, which will teach children cognitive skills which they can then transfer to other areas of the curriculum. In a sense, this is associative learning, which reflects how the brain works (Deacon, 1997; Greenfield, 1997). In our language lessons in this book, we guide children towards exploring how language works by reflecting on how the different lexical items (verbs, nouns, pronouns) are manipulated by the producer of the language. This brings me neatly to...

WHY TEACH GRAMMAR EXPLICITLY?

In the section above on the nature of explicit instruction we have already alluded to some general rationales for the beneficial effects of conscious language learning via explicit teaching: language is one of many cognitive functions;

general learning mechanisms may apply to language learning processes; conscious and reflective language learning may assist the development of other cognitive skills.

In this section we want to look for evidence that explicit instruction of grammar does promote language development in the instructional context. We will consider some general principles of language development in our search for evidence in both the L1 and L2 literature studies.

Why intervene directly to teach grammatical knowledge to L1 learners?

It may be fair to ask whether the nativists' position on language acquisition had any influence on the invisible pedagogy (Bernstein, 1975) which permeated teaching ideology in primary classrooms. This invisible pedagogy was characterised by no direct instruction and no intervention in the child's own construction of the world. We have seen that according to the nativists children received no instruction from their parents. Yet they learned language surprisingly well, and with amazing speed. However, let us look at some counter arguments.

- It is not true that young children receive no instructional input from their parents or other adults in the early stages of language acquisition. This was the whole basis for Chomsky's (1957, 1965) proposition of a language acquisition device (LAD). Chomsky based his theories not on empirical evidence but on the assumption that children turn out to be remarkably competent at language construction in spite of inadequate information they receive. However, there is substantial evidence that adults provide infants and growing children with syntactical information during conversational interactions (Baker and Nelson, 1984); Bohannon and Stanowicz, 1988; Cross, 1978; Demetras et al, 1986; Farrar, 1992; Hoff-Ginsberg, 1990; Nelson et al, 1973; Nelson 1977.

  They do this mainly by expanding and recasting children's malformed utterances into well-formed adult models (as decribed on p.20: recasts and expansions). Even though children may not take up the correct information at the time that this modelling is provided, this does not justify the assumption that the adult modelling does not affect their language development. As children learn to use the stimuli they receive in the input their subsequent responses may reveal evidence of associative learning (Staats, 1971).

  Children will acquire verbs, for instance, according to the way they hear them used in their mothers' speech to them (Naigles and Hoff-Ginsberg, 1998). Some verbs appear earlier than others in children's utterances and this propensity mirrors the verbs' frequency in mothers' speech addressed to children. What's more, children use verbs in exactly the same way as mothers do: transitive verbs are followed by objects whereas intransitive verbs do not contain objects in children's speech, in the above mentioned study. In other words, children appear to listen for cues in mothers' speech in order to bootstrap into grammatical categories (Shi et al, 1998). They listen for phonological clues – like length of syllables – and acoustic cues – change in pitch. These cues seem to help the children decide which words they hear may be a function word – that, the, on etcetera – or a lexical word, like a noun, or a verb or an adjective. Young children don't think in grammatical terms, of course. Imagine a three-year-old's mind going 'there goes another irregular verb'! But they seem to use words with increasing accuracy as far as their grammatical productions suggest. It seems safe to assume that the way the linguistic input is constructed for them and transmitted to them will affect children's growing syntactical control.

Nursery school age children, for instance, are able to respond positively to, and learn from, a prolonged training programme on verb learning, particularly if they are told when a verb has been wrongly understood by them (Saxton et al, 1998). Relative pronouns, too, can be learned by children between the ages of three and a half and four and a half under explicit training conditions (Roth, 1984). Furthermore, the stage of cognitive development and the level of language competence makes no difference to the positive effects of grammar instruction (Cole et al, 1990). In Cole et al's study explicit instruction promotes language skills in both groups of children: those with equal language and cognitive skill development and those whose language may be well below cognitive skills. Older primary children's literacy – measured in spelling and reading gains over two years – improved dramatically in Years 3 and 4 in a cohort of primary schools (Scott et al, 1998). Following a two-year programme of multi-media structured approach to language learning spelling improved on average by twenty months and reading by twenty-three months.

• Language development is not linear (Karmiloff-Smith, 1985). It passes through stages, levels and phases simultaneously, in much the same way as learning develops in other domains. When children encounter new linguistic information, they treat it as a unique unit with no relation to anything they've heard before. This unit is treated by the children only in relation to the stimulus that provided it. For example, the word cat has a meaning in the first instance because it is accompanied by a particular picture. This is phase one. Then children look for and make functional links with other linguistic information that they have already stored. So the cat now begins to be associated with a pronoun and the child starts to refer to the animal as he or it. This is phase two. At phase three children tap the stored information and match it to the new input in order to control and monitor their own production in a discourse.

This three-phase learning can happen at any age (developmental stage) and at any level of specific knowledge acquisition. In language, whenever children are presented with new linguistic structure, like the future tense in this book (chapter 3), they will approach the learning in this way. I would suggest that in the classroom these phases may be assisted and speeded up by the reflective approach that we advocate.

*   Metalinguistic abilities – in the sense that children may instinctively know when something is right or wrong – develop during the middle school years, between the ages of 4/5-8/9. But children, it seems, cannot explain why they've made certain grammatical judgements. (Hakes, 1980; O'Donnell et al, 1967).

*   Finally, explicit grammar teaching may assist our pupils to attain 'equity' in the information-driven world in which they live (Kress and Knapp, 1992). These authors suggest that if we assume that 'all members of a society have the fullest understanding of the principles underlying the production of meaning through language', then we would wish to endeavour that 'all children growing into that kind of society have the fullest understanding and competence in the production and use of information in language' (p.11).

Why teach explicit grammar to L2 learners?

In the wake of L1 studies which demonstrated that there is an order in the way grammatical structures are acquired by young children – i.e. some structures are acquired before others – (Brown and Bellugi, 1964; Brown, 1973), the linguists' attention turned towards second language learning. Brown's and Brown and Bellugi's studies were observational and focused on the speech patterns produced by three very young American children.

Second language acquisition studies revealed that there is an acquisitional order here too (Dulay and Burt, 1974c, 1974d).

The order of morphemes in the acquisition of English as a second language did not mirror exactly Brown's EL1 order: the important finding was that there is an order. These findings had great impact on second language teaching in the classroom. This was particularly the case in classrooms where bilingual children were in a minority. It was advocated, therefore, that it was not necessary to teach the linguistic system to bilingual children (Dulay and Burt, 1973), because they would pick it up anyway. Comprehensible input was all that was needed (Krashen, 1985, 1987) and children would monitor their own learning by filtering out whatever irregularities they encountered in the input which did not match their hypotheses about the grammatical system of the language they were acquiring. Learning, Krashen said, was only useful if it could assist acquisition. And of course, Krashen may be right in this respect, if by acquisition we mean implicit learning.

This approach was compounded by the critical age hypothesis (Singleton and Lengyel, eds, 1995) which posited that it is difficult, if not impossible, to attain native-like proficiency after the age of 12-14 years. However both theoretical positions have been strongly challenged by applied linguists and psycholinguists as well as cognitive psychologists. First of all, there is no consensus on what native-like proficiency means. Which native-like proficiency should second language learners aspire to? A localised dialectical code – Black Vernacular English (Labov, 1972) or the standardised dialectical code American English? The expressive and imagery-rich Liverpudlian, or Standard English? Why shouldn't second language learners be given the privilege to learn both? Secondly, assuming that a notion of native-likeness could be agreed upon, there is some evidence that age may be a barrier to the acquisition of accent and pronunciation, but an advantage to grammar learning (Martohardjono and Flynn, 1995). Young children do pick up accents and pronunciation very quickly, but this may have more to do with their phonological perception than with superior language learning abilities.

It makes better sense to think in terms of assisting second language learners to attain a degree of automaticity in their processing of second language learning. The early stages of second language acquisition are characterised by a developing linguistic system known as interlanguage. At this stage emerging bilinguals are constructing a hypothesis from two linguistic systems: the L1 which they already know and the L2 which they are currently learning. In other words, they will try and work out the correct rules of the L2 in two ways:

- They will listen for patterns and regularities in the L2 input and generate rules for the L2. In such case, they may overgeneralise rules just like children do when acquiring their L1. For example they will say things like I comed.

- If they can't find a structure in the L2 knowledge they have already acquired (because they have not met it, or they have forgotten it) they will look for a similar construction in their L1 which would translate what they want to say in the L2. For example, to say 'this coffee isn't hot' in Italian, one would say 'questo caffè non è caldo'. To express the negative in Italian, the negation non comes before the verb è, which means is. In English the negation comes after the verb. At the interlanguage stage Italians learning English may very well say 'this coffee not is hot' until they have, either discovered by themselves the correct rule for expressing negation in English, or until somebody teaches it to them, informally in conversation or in an instructional context.

So to achieve the stage of automatic processing and production, second language learners have to go from this interlanguage through a process of automatisation to automaticity. This process is continuous (De Keyser, 1997). There is no dichotomy of no-second-language at one end of a continuum and automaticity at the other end. It is a tortuous process of non-linear progression. This is probably assisted and speeded up by a combination of explicit instruction and varying models of general learning mechanisms, like the instance theory of learning (Logan, 1992). This model suggests that the mind reacts faster each time an item, which is the focus of learning, is presented. Thus the learning is fine-tuned, reaction-time gets shorter and shorter, errors diminish and eventually processing and production become automatic.

> ... the sequence of explicit rule learning, followed by a short period of activities focused on using explicit knowledge during performance of target skills, and finally by a long period of repeated opportunities to use that knowledge, is likely to yield knowledge that is highly automatised (De Keyser, 1997 p215).

Explicit learning may not, of course, work on its own in pursuit of automaticity. Implicit learning, the natural acquisition process – which can develop slowly over a long period of time if left to its own device – does contribute to the attainment of automaticity. In fact, implicit and explicit learning may be mutually supportive. Enhanced by explicitly instructed learning, the process is speeded up (Robinson, 1997).

A great deal of investigation into the effects of explicit instruction on second language learning has been carried out in authentic instructional contexts as well as in laboratory conducted experiments with artificial languages. The learners in the investigations vary in age and educational levels – from primary school children to university students and non-student adults. The findings are interesting. There seems to be a consensus that instruction is better than no instruction (MacWhinney, 1997). The instructional approaches may vary considerably, as we have indicated already earlier – see the table on page 15.

In the HOW section below are brief résumés of some of these studies, both from L1 and L2 literature. These represent a much greater body of literature (especially in the area of second language acquisition) which has been investigating the effects of varying degrees of explicit instruction on language development.

HOW TO TEACH EXPLICIT GRAMMAR

Twelve résumés of a variety of explicit instructions are presented in the tables below to give an overview of research findings. There are seven studies with children ranging from nursery school age to 11+. Four of the children's studies focus on their first (L1) language learning, in all cases here it is English. Three of the children's studies investigate their learning of a second language. Five studies focus on adults learning a second language. Although in this book we are concerned with teaching English in primary classrooms, there is much that we can adapt from an adult approach to the primary classroom, and vice versa. A

Summary of explicit strategies used with children in both L1 and L2 studies	Summary of strategies used with adults in L2 learning studies
• Highly structured stimulus material, e.g. pictures, puppets, toys with which to present and illustrate grammatical structures	• Text presentation containing targeted grammatical structures; pictures and cartoons
• Systematic presentation of structures	• Systematic presentation of structures
• Enact grammatical structure with toys	• Demonstrate use of structures
• Elicit imitation from children: guided conversation and repetition	• Elicited comprehension: questions designed so that learners' answers contain grammar structure
• Ask children questions in such a way that children's answers have to include grammatical structure	• Text manipulation: e.g. sentence construction and deconstruction
• Play games	• Enhancing input: e.g. highlighting, underlining
• Elicit comprehensible output: emphasis on meaning	• Metalinguistic explanation of structures
• Highlighting words, phrases, sentences	• Problem solving activities
• Problem solving activities	• Grammaticality judgements
• Plenty of practice	• Plenty of practice
• Elicit grammaticality judgements from children	• Corrective feedback
• Give corrective feedback	

comparison of the strategies used with children and with adults in these studies will illustrate similarities in approaches.

Each résumé in the tables is self-explanatory, including the theoretical frameworks, in the third column, which have been discussed in this chapter. In our own teaching of grammar we have not focused on the type of feedback one should give in the classroom to effect appropriate language behaviour. Some of the studies indicate that there is a significant role which different types of feedback play in language learning. Feedback is an integral part of the whole teaching approach. We inform children, in one way or another, about the state of their performance, be it aural, oral or written. However, in the grammar lessons in this book we have not indicated any form of feedback. We have concentrated on raising children's awareness of language investigation so as to exert some control on their own output.

TEACHING STRATEGIES from RESEARCH LITERATURE

L1 instructional context – Children

Author/s and date	Study	Theoretical Framework
Roth 1984	**Experiment – 3 weeks** To test effects of direct intervention on child's comprehension of relative clauses, which may still be beyond children's developmental grasp **Study groups –** • explicit training • implicit training • control (no training of relative clauses; exposure to and enactment of conjoined sentences) **Age/Educational level/ L1** 18 children between ages 3:6 and 4:6. English L1 **Strategies – Explicit condition** • verbal presentation to children of sentence containing main and relative clause with toys • enact sentence to the child • separate main and relative clauses into two sentences • ask child to enact both sentences **Strategies – Implicit condition** • present the complete sentences • child asked to enact the sentence **Strategies – control condition** • child taught to act out conjoined sentences **Indications –** • Training does affect learning of relative clauses; groups 1 and 2 outperformed control group and improved between pre-test and post-test • training does not affect the children's pre-existing disposition to process more easily subject relative noun phrase than object relative clause.	Language Learning Can be Pushed Beyond Current Cognitive Development
Saxton *et al* 1998	**Experiment – 5 weeks** Effects of understanding and retention of past tense of two instructional methods – positive input only; a mixture of positive, negative and corrective input **Study groups** All children received same training; variability tested by teaching 2 nonsense verbs differently: • verb 1 – positive input only • verb 2 – positive + negative + corrective feedback **Age/Educational level/L1** 26 children, mean age 3:10; nursery school; English L1 **Strategies – Verbs 1 and 2 in training session** • teach base form + -ing form of verbs with puppets • children asked to identify verbs in line drawing • elicit use of verbs by children via questions and answers using pictures **Strategies – Verb 1 past tense** • demonstrate past tense with glove puppets • create a scenario with puppets • comment on what has happened – eg. *ask did you see?* *The spider pulled the grasshopper* (p710)	Language Learning Can be Accelerated By Manipulation Of Input

TEACHING STRATEGIES from RESEARCH LITERATURE (continued)

L1 instructional context – Children

Author/s and date	Study	Theoretical Framework
	• child responds • encourage child further eg. *is that right? Can you tell me what happened?* (p.710) **Strategies – Verb 2 past tense** • demonstrate tense with puppets • create scenario • ask child to say what happened • child produces incorrect verb response • correct child by providing correct verb in expanded sentence **Post-test grammaticality judgements –** Using puppets create scenarios. A dragon says what has happened. Children reward dragon if it said verb correctly **Indications** THREE TYPES OF INPUT USED TOGETHER -POSITIVE EVIDENCE + NEGATIVE EVIDENCE + CORRECTIVE FEEDBACK – facilitate, accelerate and assist retention of language learning	
Cole *et al* 1990	**Experiment – one year** To test effects of two instruction programmes on language learning when language and cognitive skills are on the same level of development: academically-based programme designed for learners whose language skills are below cognitive skills; non-commercial cognitive-based programme. **Study groups –** • CR group – Cognitive Referencing i.e. with language levels below cognitive skills • CAR – Chronological Age Referencing i.e. cognitive and linguistic development on a par **Age/Educational Level/L1** Pre-school; group 1 mean age 4:11, group 2 5:3; English L1 **Strategies – Academic Programme** • extensive task analysis of structures to be taught • systematic presentation of structures to be taught • pre-task elicited imitation • rapid pace • highly structured stimulus materials **Strategies – Cognitive-based Programme** • no elicited imitation • modelling • child-directed conversation – natural context • slower pace • naturally occurring reinforcement **Indications** INSTRUCTION affects language performance of all children, whose linguistic and cognitive development may or not be on a par.	**Language Is a Function Of General Cognition**

TEACHING STRATEGIES from RESEARCH LITERATURE (continued)

L1 instructional context – Children

Author/s and date	Study	Theoretical
Scott *et al* 1998	**Evaluation – 2 year study** Effects of multimedia structured approach to language teaching and learning on literacy skills, spelling and reading **Groups** Year 3 and Year 4 classes **Age/Educational level/L1** Approximately between ages 7-9; primary school; English L1 **Strategies** • emphasis on meaning • highlighting words, phrases, sentences • speed reading • multi-sensory phonics teaching • talking dictionary • systematic teaching of new concepts and vocabulary • parrot Mode imitation • problem solving activities **Indications** HIGHLY STRUCTURED LANGUAGE TEACHING leads to significant improvement in reading (average by 23 months over two years) and spelling (average 20 months over two years).	**Instruction and literacy development**

L2 instructional context – Children

Harley 1989	**Experiment – 8 weeks** Effects of explicit teaching of difficult grammatical structures (here the French imparfait/continuous past and the passe' compose'/perfect tense) in an analytical-functional approach on grammatical development **Study group –** One class only **Age/educational level/L1 and L2** Approximately age 11 +; grade 6; English L1; French L2, total immersion **Strategies –** • train teachers: on grammatical structures, prepared materials and how to use them *in class:* • read: story containing the targeted structure • test comprehension: of structures in the story by asking questions containing those structures • text manipulation: by pupils working in teams • interpretation/inference: of aspects expressed in text: in small groups • guided sentence construction: with photos and captions • guided oral production: story-based and own-experience based • games: miming/guessing • guided story-writing: with pictures and incomplete sentences/story • guided creative writing: drawing on original story • judging story: by peers for correct grammatical use of targeted structures • reconstruct jigsaw story: and insert correct verb tense	**Functional Aspects of Language In Teaching Programme**

TEACHING STRATEGIES from RESEARCH LITERATURE (continued)

L2 instructional context – Children

Author/s and date	Study	Theoretical

Spada and Lightbown 1993	**Experiment – in classroom – two weeks + 3 post tests:**
	Post-test 1 – immediately after treatment
	Post-test 2 – $2^1/_2$ weeks later
	Post test 3 – $3^1/_2$ months later
	Effect of explicit form-focused instruction and corrective feedback on the development of interrogative constructions
	Study groups –
	• explicit instruction + explicit corrective feedback
	• explicit instruction + implicit corrective feedback
	• control – (a non-experiment teacher's interaction with the pupils is analysed in its own right to categorise grammar teaching and feedback)
	Age/educational level/L1 and L2 –
	10-12 years old; French L1; English L2
	Strategies –
	• focus-on-forms – oral communication tasks:
	    • look at set of pictures –
	    • questions: by students to interviewer on attributes of interviewer's hidden picture in order to find a match in the visible set, until a match could be found –
	    • prompt by interviewer: if student unable to ask a *wh* question after first two questions
	• explicit corrective feedback
	    • metalinguistic question: to get students to focus on correct position of the verb in the question –
	    • metalinguistic rule is given –
	    • repetition with intonation rise: to signal incorrectness –
	    • outright rejection of error (no..) –
	    • paralinguistic: stress, snapping fingers, gasping
	• implicit corrective feedback: provide correct version only with no explanation or any other paralinguistics to attract attention to error
	• focus-on-form: instruction and corrective feedback is context embedded, i.e. provided in context of meaningful and sustained communicative interaction
	Indications –
	FOCUS-ON-FORMS INSTRUCTION + CORRECTIVE FEEDBACK and FOCUS-ON-FORM + CORRECTIVE FEEDBACK lead to continued improvement over five-month period in number, well-formedness and type of questions asked.
		Short-term Memory and long term language development

Lyster and Ranta 1997	**Observational study in classroom – 100hrs** Does classroom teacher-learner interaction contain types of feedback which lead to learner uptake? **Age/educational level/L1 and L2** Approximately age 9-10; four classes at grade 4, of which one class was mixed grades 4 and 5; mixture of L1s; French (immersion) L2 **Study groups –** As described above	Compre-hensible Output Hypothesis in negotiations of Meanings

TEACHING STRATEGIES from RESEARCH LITERATURE (continued)

L2 instructional context – Children

Author/s and date	Study	Theoretical
	Strategies – feedback types identified –	

• elicitation: 3 types:
> • teacher elicits completion of own utterance eg. 'it is...?'
> • teacher uses questions to elicit correct form eg. 'how do you say...?'
> • students are asked to reformulate own answers

• clarification requests: teacher asks for repetition or reformulation with phrases such as 'pardon me?'

• metalinguistic feedback: comments or questions on how well formed a student's answer is eg. 'can you find your error?', 'no, not...'

• repetition: i.e. teacher repeats student's error in isolation, often with rising intonation

Indication –

These FOUR TYPES OF FEEDBACK lead to learner uptake in L2

L2 instructional context – adults

Doughty 1991

Experiment – computer assisted – 10 days

Effects of three different instructional approaches, i.e. with focus on form, markedness and visual cues, on rule learning and rule transference

Study groups –

• MOG – meaning oriented group, with salient visual cues

• ROG – rule oriented, explicit presentation of rule + visual cues

• COG – control, exposure only to artificially high proportion of marked relative clause

Age/educational level/L1 and L2 –

No age specified; university students; several L1s with similar relativisation to English; English L2.

Strategies – of ROG group

• Skim – text sentences for content

• In-depth reading – of the whole text for understanding

• Rule learning – via animated grammar i.e. on computer screen the following sequence appears:
> • explicit rule statement
> • sentence manipulation in two parts A and B

• *Part A* – 5 steps to deconstruct a sentence and reduce it to two simple sentences (rule presented at each step)
> • identify and label relative pronoun in relative clause, and head phrase in matrix clause
> • show where relative pronoun came from and how it was replaced by a duplicate head noun
> • locate noun with respect to verb phrase
> • identify original main and relative clause
> • separate the two clauses into two simple sentences

• *Part B* – reverse the stepwise process in A: i.e. recombine the 2 simple sentences into original complete sentences with matrix and relative clauses

Pieneman's Teachability Hypothesis

Instruction is affective at the interlanguage grammar acquisition if the instruction reflects the natural order of development as revealed in the SLA literature.

TEACHING STRATEGIES from RESEARCH LITERATURE (continued)

L2 instructional context – adults

Author/s and date	Study	Theoretical

	• visual cues – in order to focus attention on the rule being taught, here relative clauses:
	   • Labelling
	   • Disappearance and replacement of linguistic elements
	   • Animated movements on the screen
	• Markedness – i.e. where the rule is most easily noticed and therefore most accessible (in this study the relative pronoun functions as the subject of the clause, therefore most easily noticed because of its markedness)
	Indications –
	EXPLICIT RULE INSTRUCTION + STEP-BY-STEP SENTENCE MANIPULATION + VISUAL CUES + MARKEDNESS leads to significant improvement in knowledge of rule and in transference of rule to other less marked relative clauses.	

Robinson and Ha 1993	**Experiment – computer assisted –** Effects of explicit rule teaching (in training session) + instance practice (learning session) + transfer (new semantic context session) on automatic grammaticality judgements with accuracy **Age/educational level/L1 and L2 –** No age specified; 15 university students; three L1s: Japanese, Korean, French; English L2 **Study groups –** One treatment group only **Strategies – training session –** • give rule: with illustration and highlighting of focus structure, here verbs that have been made up to teach verb alternation • explain important component of the rule: in this case, what a syllable is • time: unlimited time to read the rule before continuing • signal: that the rule has been understood before moving on • judge grammaticality: individual sentences on the screen to be judged correct/incorrect • immediate feedback: students are told on screen if their grammaticality judgement is correct/incorrect before moving on **Strategies – practice session –** • sentences are presented on the screen in multiple presentations in descending order: i.e. sentence number one is presented eight times, sentence number two seven times, and so on • students make grammaticality judgements on the sentences • immediate feedback is given as in the training session **Strategies – transfer session –** • random mix of old and new sentences: familiar verbs are presented in new sentences and new verbs are presented in old frames • students make grammaticality judgements as in previous sessions • immediate feedback as before	**Logan's Instance Theory of Practice** The more you practice something the shorter the reaction time is in recognising correct patterns and the more accurate and automatic the judgement will be. Automaticity is achieved via three processes on encountering a stimulus: • Encoding of stimulus • Retrieval of stimulus • Stimulus is represented in the memory as a separate instance.

TEACHING STRATEGIES from RESEARCH LITERATURE (continued)

L2 instructional context – adults

Author/s and date	Study	Theoretical
	Indications – THE MORE FREQUENT THE EXPOSURE + PRACTICE leads to faster reaction time in recall and to more accurate grammaticality judgements.	

De Graaf
1997
	Experiment – laboratory – 10 weeks – 1½hr per week
	Computer assisted learning of artificial language (Esperanto) to test the effects of explicit instruction + immediate feedback on L2 acquisition
	Study groups –
	• explicit instruction
	• implicit instruction
	Both groups receive self-study packs with exact features of activities and aids, eg. translation in Dutch
	Age/educational level/L1 and L2 –
	No age specified; university students, non-linguists, though one foreign language had been studied at secondary school; Dutch L1; Esperanto L2
	Strategies – explicit instruction –
	• understand a text: eg. read a dialogue and carry out comprehension (question and answer) task
	• explanation: of grammatical structures in the text to focus on forms and their syntactic meaning
	• feedback on every item, i.e.
	    • inform on correctness
	    • students asked to repeat corrected sentence
	    • short grammatical explanation after feedback
	Strategies – implicit instruction –
	• read dialogue
	• comprehension activities
	• rehearsal of unordered examples of sentences
	• feedback with no grammatical explanation
	Indications –
	EXPLICIT INSTRUCTION + IMMEDIATE EXPLANATORY FEEDBACK leads to second language acquisition
		Grammatical consciousness and developing explicit L2 Knowledge
		
		Explicit versus implicit instruction and noticing as a pedagogical tool to assist development of L2 explicit knowledge.

De Keyser 1997	**Experiment – laboratory** Computer assisted learning of an artificial language (Autopractan) to test effects of explicit instruction + explicit feedback + detailed grammatical explanation + practice on attaining automaticity in L2 **Study groups –** Three groups received the same method of instruction and presentation of four rules of grammar and vocabulary in the first 5 sessions and the same test in session 6, followed by 15 practice sessions, each group practising the rules in different ways: see strategies below **Age/educational level/L1 and L2 –** No age specified; university students; English L1; Autopractan L2	**ACT Model Of Learning** **A**daptive **C**ontrol of **T**hought is a three staged process of automatisation which leads to automaticity: • declarative knowledge is interpreted

TEACHING STRATEGIES from RESEARCH LITERATURE (continued)

L2 instructional context – adults

Author/s and date	Study	Theoretical

	Strategies –
	• traditional grammar presentation (2 sessions): vocabulary with pictures, and question and answer comprehension
	• recall (3 sessions): random order of vocabulary items and students required to fill blanks which test explicit rule knowledge
	• test (1 session)
	• 15 practice sessions:
	    Group A – practised only two rules in each of the two practice activities i.e. comprehension and production
	    Group B – practised same as A, but the rules were reversed i.e. those in comprehension for A were in production for B and vice versa
	    Group C – all 4 rules in each of production and comprehension
	Indications –
	EXPLICIT INSTRUCTION OF RULES + EXPLICIT FEEDBACK + DETAILED GRAMMATICAL EXPLANATION + PRACTICE leads to automaticity in L2
	NB. *Practice leads to highly specific skills* i.e. the practice sessions allowed for differentiated time being spent on each rule in either comprehension or production; more practice in comprehension leads to better performance in comprehension, and more practice in production leads to better performance.
		• knowledge is compiled into forms of procedures
		• ongoing fine tuning of procedures

Robinson 1997	**Experiment – computer assisted –** Effects of 4 different types of instruction (implicit, incidental, enhanced, instructed) on generalizability and automaticity after four sessions of work: practice session, training, transfer and debriefing sessions **Study groups –** • implicit treatment – (subjects told to remember position of words in sentences which they would meet in reading exercises) • incidental – (focus on meaning and understanding) • enhanced – (focus on meaning, understanding and visual cues, eg. framed in a box, to draw attention to forms and their rules) • instructed **Age/educational level/L1 and L2 –** 19-24 years old; university students; Japanese L1; English L2 **Strategies – instructed group -practice session –** • introduction: to method of instruction • metalinguistic explanation of the rule: 2/3 minutes – illustrated with written materials • students asked to remember the rule and refer to it in the written materials if needed during the training session • practise: three sentences as per sequence below in training session **Strategies – training session – 25 minutes –** • read sentences with rules (10 seconds each)	**Noticing hypothesis and Logan's Instance theory of Automaticity** Noticing hypothesis says that what learners notice in input becomes intake in learning. Instance theory says: • Each time solutions are found to a problem is an instance • Instances accumulate in memory

TEACHING STRATEGIES from RESEARCH LITERATURE (continued)

L2 instructional context – adults

Author/s and date	Study	Theoretical
	• answer metalinguistic question: on each sentence (as much time as wanted/needed) • students are reminded on screen that the sentences just seen were grammatical and that they would now see new sentences **Strategies – transfer session – 2/5 minutes** • read: 30 sentences are presented in random order (first 2 sentences are distractors to give time to get familiar with new activity) • decide: if they are grammatical or not **Strategies – debriefing session –** • had any rules been noticed by the students? • had they been looking for rules? • could they say what the rules were? **Indications –** EXPLICIT RULE TEACHING leads to higher accuracy and faster reaction time in judging grammatical/ungrammatical, old and new sentences; therefore TRANSFER OF KNOWLEDGE leads to generalisability and automaticity.	• Performance is a result of retrieval of these memories.

CHAPTER 2

COLLABORATIVE LEARNING AND VERBS

Susan Moule

Parkgate JM School, Watford, Hertfordshire

THE SCHOOL

Parkgate JM school is a county school in Watford, England. Two hundred and forty children attend and they are divided into eight mixed ability classes, two classes in each year group. The pupils come from a wide range of social and cultural backgrounds. They provide a rich resource in themselves as the children are encouraged to work harmoniously and use their knowledge from their lives outside school to enhance their work in school.

The Section 11 teacher helps to develop an understanding throughout the school of the cultural diversities among the pupils at Parkgate JM school. A quarter of the pupils are from a variety of ethnic communities. About forty children in the school speak English as an additional language, their first languages being Panjabi, Urdu, Bengali or Gujerati.

The introduction of the National Literacy Strategy together with the New Orders made all teachers look again at the curriculum. At the school where I teach we have been keen to use these government directives to enrich and enhance the work that we already do. The strategies developed and presented here incorporate my school's existing ideologies while embracing innovative ways of teaching the English language to all the children in our classes. I hope that you will be able to use the strategies described in this chapter to fit in with, and extend, your existing pool of ideas and resources.

INTRODUCTION TO LANGUAGE LEARNING BY TWO YEAR 4 CLASSES – 1996/97 and 1997/98

This part of the book describes language work with two very different classes in two separate academic years. When I first came across the collaborative learning approach in the autumn term of 1996 I was about to start working on a writing project with my class so that the children could develop an awareness of different writing genres. This was an integral part of the school's and the national curriculum KS2 requirements.

I decided to experiment with this approach to learning. It seemed to me that it might provide me and my pupils with a firmer structure of work than we were used to, though I must confess that the task seemed daunting at the time! At first sight it seems that collaborative learning is only suited to project-type work which requires, by its very nature, a research-based approach to learning and therefore invites group discussions. In addition a project provides continuity and the opportunity for individuals and groups to work and learn together over a period thus, possibly, enhancing the quality of the learned outcome. However, I wanted to find out if this approach is transferable. Would it work in a one-off lesson? Would it work with a different type of language work?

The second adaptation of collaborative learning presented here is the grammar work with my Year 4 class of 1997-1998. Fulfilling the requirements of the National Curriculum KS2 (DFE, 1995, p 16) and those of the National Literacy hour (DfEE, 1998, p 43), the past tense was the area of grammar I selected for this class. There follows a detailed account of two sequences of lessons in which the teaching is so structured that the children truly collaborate in their learning:

- a six-lesson project on different writing genres – where each lesson is a continuation of the previous one

- a three-session investigation of the past tense – three lessons each of which can stand on its own

But first I would like to justify why I chose collaborative learning in the first place. My aims were:

- to teach children to work together.

- to use collaborative learning as a vehicle to increase literacy, as well as the speaking and listening skills of all the children: in 1996-97 I did this by providing groups of four children with examples of different genres of writing which they would study and use in their own writing together bouncing ideas off each other.

- as a tool for classroom management, by providing children with challenging but step-by-step work, so that they would be fully aware of expectations. This enabled me to spend more time with groups, extending a range of literacy and collaborative skills.

The skills needed for collaborative work are valuable in everyday life. Collaborative work can be used to enhance work across the curriculum.

THE WRITING PROJECT WITH YEAR 4 1996-98
WRITING A MINI SAGA

This project was devised with the following goals in mind:

- so that the children could develop an awareness of different styles of writing, each one requiring a particular mental and linguistic approach

- so that the children could appreciate that creative writing and reportage are not always solitary occupations but often the result of a team of people collaborating in the writing as, for example, on a film script

- to teach the children that writing is a developmental process that needs planning.

I decided that this project had to be a staged development during which all the necessary sequence of planning a piece of writing – whatever it might be – would become apparent. Five phases were devised for this project, each concentrating on one or two aspects of writing a saga. Each phase might have more than one lesson. I hoped that by writing a mini saga, the children would develop and maintain a piece of extended writing by focusing on essential themes such as characterisation and setting while at the same time appreciating their effect on the quality of the writing.

Phase One – lessons 1 and 2

The first part of this project involved getting the children to think of the main ingredients of a story and the different ways a story can be told i.e. in a poem, a cartoon strip, a diary, a letter and so on. The next important step was for the children to become accustomed to working in small collaborative groups. They had to understand precisely what this involves and why each member of the group had an important role to play in the cohesive work of the group. They also needed to appreciate that each group in the class was going to play a specific role in this investigative project. Roles were allocated to the individual children in each group: scribe, spellchecker, chairperson and reporter – the person who reported to the class on the progress and findings of the group's work.

Each group was responsible for investigating one style of writing. We studied eight styles, so formed eight groups:

- the cartoon group

- the poetry group

- the play group

- the picture-book group

- the diary group

- the story-told-in-chapters group

- the short story group

- the newspaper group

The intended outcome of this phase was for the children to understand what a saga is and for each group to produce its own definition of a saga. It was important that the children understood the idea of saga, because future work would be based around their understanding of the term. This phase also introduced the idea of working collaboratively. The scene for future work was set early on, giving the children some experience on which to base their expectations of what was to come.

Phase Two – lesson 3

The groups were to make critical appraisals of different styles of writing and produce a list of words which identify a particular style. We began by looking at characterisation. This generated a character outline for the stories which each group would write in the allocated style of writing. Providing texts with task sheets to look at encouraged the children to focus on aspects of the structure and style of their texts. Again, my aim was to provide foundations of experience on which children could build their future activities in the project.

Phase Three – lesson 4

The groups would study a second aspect of story writing: the setting. Each group would have to end the session with a setting to match the story line and the characters, which were by now taking shape in their minds. One aim was to look at a different aspect of texts each session, whilst still pointing out the links between elements of characterisation, setting and genre. I wanted the children to realise that each element was important in its own right and how it could be used to enhance the quality of writing. I hoped they would get a feel for their stories and where they were heading. Although each session focused on a different element of the story, they worked within the same framework for collaboration.

Phase Four – lesson 5

Consider one last ingredient essential to a good story: the events. Using their notes on characterisation and setting, they would begin to pull it all together by producing, by the end of this session, a first draft of events taking place in certain settings, involving all or some of the characters already invented.

Phase Five – lesson 6

One lesson to make a start; more time would be needed to complete the work.

The intended outcomes are eight sagas, to include all the features discussed: characters, settings, events. Each saga written in one of the eight styles to be studied during the course of the programme.

The lesson plans which follow are reproduced as they were written, in the present tense.

Summary

This writing project was underpinned by a step-by-step approach during which the children would learn a number of new skills essentially to:

- learn to collaborate with their peers on a project which, in real life, often requires team co-operation

- learn to plan and produce a piece of writing by first deciding on the intended audience.

Learning to write for an intended audience was structured along developmental stages of learning

- decide on the audience: this dictates the style one should write in

- study the different styles of writing

- once a style is chosen to tell a story, study the ingredients of the story and how each should be written in the selected style of writing

- the ingredients for a good story were looked at in this sequence: characterisation, settings and events

- the production of the story, adhering to the planned framework.

CLASS 4 OF 1996-1997
BIOGRAPHICAL DETAILS and PROFILE

Number of pupils: 30
Number of pupils who have EAL (English as an Additional Language): 4
Languages spoken: English and Urdu
Ability Level: National Curriculum level 3 – 4 in English

General delivery of the curriculum:
Subject-based lessons. I used whole-class teaching with provision for individual, pair and group work within the framework of a lesson.

Physical environment:
Seated in groups of four or six children, mostly in mixed ability, though sometimes according to ability for certain subjects.

The class consisted of many strong characters and leaders – suitable for collaborative learning. I wanted to provide opportunities for all children to experience the whole range of roles when working with others and not just let a few children dominate. This proved quite a challenge and initially there were problems with group dynamics. But as the children became more used to this way of working the problems began to subside.

Phase One – Lesson One – Defining a saga – 50 minutes

Language focus – vocabulary needed to describe a saga, especially adjectives

Aims

• to define what saga means

• to sort the class into their groups

• to decide what makes a saga

Materials

Board, paper, pencils, dictionaries.

Roles needed for collaborative group work in this lesson

Scribe, spellchecker, chairperson, reporter

Lesson

20 minutes whole class – teacher-led discussion

• ask the children to name their favourite television programmes

• when a child mentions a soap opera, ask the children to say what type of programme this is – keep eliciting more descriptions until they come up with the term soap opera

• introduce the term saga as a similar word

• talk about books they might have read that could be defined as sagas eg. The Famous Five

• discuss why these books are sagas – encourage the children to realise issues such as:

  – all stories have main characters

  – authors generally describe the main characters fully

• ask the children to think of soap operas in a similar way

10 minutes group allocation

• tell the children that they are going to be working in small groups of four

• each child in each group will need to work closely with the rest of the group – meaning listening to the others, discussing and respecting what the others say

- allocate the children to the groups and tell them the names for each group, i.e. cartoon group, poetry group and so on

10 minutes group discussion
- the groups to discuss what makes a saga and to come up with their own definitions

10 minutes whole class – feedback
- each group's reporter to read the group's definition to the rest of the class

Evaluation of this lesson

Initially the children seemed a little unsure and rather apprehensive. This is understandable. We all remember that daunting feeling of doing something new, or being asked to work with people we do not know well. This is why I chose the groups and the children's roles within the groups – to try and provide some stability and fairness – and in the hope that no one would feel excluded.

The children needed some time to settle into this way of working. Some needed reassurance that their own role was important to the group, others needed to know that they would have opportunities to try out other roles in future lessons. They also needed guidance on how to sort out minor disagreements and work harmoniously and democratically. A tall order for anyone – let alone children aged 8-9. However, all these reservations are in themselves justifications for doing such work.

This was a very pleasing outcome of the first attempt at truly collaborative work by this class. Five definitions, resulting from the eight groups' discussions of what a saga is, are given below.

Saga
A saga is a story that carries on in a series.
There are characters that carry on in every chapter.
A saga could be like a soap opera
And it is a
story

Sagas
Sagas are a bit like soap operas.
Sagas are stories.
Books can be sagas.
A series of books is a saga.
They have the same characters throughout.
Sagas carry a story on for a long time.
Sagas are usually interesting adventures.
Sagas can be mysterious, funny and sometimes sad.
Sagas are cliff-hangers.
Television sagas are made in studios.

A Saga

A saga can be believable.
A saga must have the same characters all the way through.
A saga is realistic.
A saga is interesting.
At the end of an episode there is always a cliff-hanger
to make people want to watch it again.

A Saga

A saga is a long story.
Every episode ends in a cliff-hanger.
Animals can be in sagas as well as humans.

Saga

Characters are the same throughout the story.
Sagas are long stories.
Each part ends on a cliff-hanger.
Every part is different.
It can be funny and must be interesting.

Lesson 2 – looking at styles of writing – 50 minutes

Language focus – the author's use of language which finally
characterises that style

Aims

*   for the children to look at styles of writing in eight different formats:
    cartoon, poem, play, diary, chapter-story, short story, newspaper and picture
    book

*   for the children to decide how each author presents the characters and story
    line

*   for the children to look critically at the language the author uses to attract
    and hold the reader's attention and interest

Materials

Eight different examples of writing to give to each group:

*   a cartoon strip to the cartoon group – Mr. Wolf's week by Colin Hawkins

*   a poem to the poetry group – Dog in the playground by Alan Ahlberg

*   a diary page to the diary group

*   a newspaper page to the newspaper group

- a story in chapters to the story-in-chapters group

- a picture book to the picture-book group – Watch out, Bernard

- a Sainsbury's Changing picture book

- a play to the play group

[These materials are used again throughout the project as needed and especially in lesson 4, Phase 3]

Roles needed for this lesson

The groups are divided into two pairs in each group, with one reader in each group and the group's reporter.

Lesson

15 minutes whole class – teacher-led discussion
- the children sit in their working groups and distribute their task sheets

- discuss the task sheet with the whole class

- ask individual children to read bits of it and make sure they all understand all the vocabulary and ideas in it: eg.

  characters – what is a character?

  setting – what does this mean and what is it in a story?

  improve – can the children give an example?

- distribute the appropriate reading materials to the groups i.e. cartoon strips to the cartoon group and so on

20 minutes pair work
- two children in each group to read the group's allocated reading genre and complete the task sheet

- each pair to discuss with the other pair in the group the aspects they have noticed about their group's particular writing genre

- the group to decide on its own definitive group's findings

15 minutes whole class
- plenary with each group's reporter presenting the characteristics of the particular writing style analysed by the group

The groups' task sheet and their findings on characteristics of different writing styles are presented below. This lesson's work revealed some strengths (what worked) and weaknesses (what didn't work) in the content of the lesson and the task sheet prepared for the class. This was evidenced by the outcome, i.e. how

Lesson 2
GROUPS' TASK SHEET
Looking at styles of writing

- Underline the style of writing that you are looking at:
  Diary, newspaper, play, cartoon, picture book, a story told in chapters, a poem, a short story

- How does the story begin? Think about how the author introduces us to the characters and the setting of the story.

- Does the author ever include himself/herself in the writing by using 'I'?

- Underline the correct words which best describe the piece of writing that you are looking at (you may underline more than one word).
  Funny, sad, scary, exciting, happy, serious.

- How else would you describe this story?

- Find your three favourite words in the piece of writing that you are looking at.

- How do they help to improve the piece of writing?

- If you are looking at the picture book, describe part of your favourite picture and how this helps you tell the story.

the children described the different writing styles following the instructions and questions in the task sheet. My observations on this are given below, after the children's findings.

Comments on the task sheet

This task sheet was designed to get the children to focus on styles of writing by directing them to consider various features.

All the groups answered the first question. Though their answers are fairly minimal, they seem to appreciate the idea of a main character. The group looking at the play appreciate how the characters are listed but not how the author builds up a picture of them. None of the groups tackled the idea of characterisation nor description of setting. This could be because the question was too 'global' – a text-focused question on character and setting might have encouraged fuller responses.

The groups were able to understand that writing can evoke different emotions. But the question 'How else would you describe this story?' may need refining depending upon the age and ability of the children. Only three groups provided a satisfactory answer. Question of this type were beyond the ability of some groups.

No group answered 'How do they help to improve the piece of writing?' about their three favourite words in their text. This suggests that the children did not see the links between these two questions – that the words they chose might have been used to develop characters and settings, or to make the story funnier, sadder and so on. So although this task sheet was designed to help structure the children's ideas, it actually provided valuable for assessment.

Outcome of lesson 2
LOOKING AT WRITING STYLES
The different groups' findings

How does the story begin? Think about how the author introduces us to the characters and the setting of the story

Cartoon	The main character is shown walking in the rain
Poem	The main characters are introduced on the first line
Play	The names of the main characters are listed in the order of what they say
Picture book	We're introduced to the first character on the first page
Diary group	We are first told the setting is on a ship and there are nine people with the captain
Story told in chapters	The author introduces Flash Harriet and where she lives
Short story	The story starts when the author introduces the characters in pictures
Newspaper	The story begins with a headline; that tells you who the characters are and where it takes place

Does the author ever include himself/herself in the writing by using 'I'?

Cartoon	No
Poem	No
Play	Yes
Picture book	No
Diary group	Yes
Story told in chapters	Yes
Short story	Sometimes
Newspaper	No

Underline the words which best describe the piece of writing that you are looking at (you may underline more than one word)

Funny, sad, scary, exciting, happy, serious.

Cartoon	Funny and exciting
Poem	Funny, sad and exciting
Play	Funny, sad, exciting, happy and serious
Picture book	Funny and exciting
Diary	Sad, scary serious
Story told in chapters	Funny, exciting and happy
Short story	Funny, scary and exciting
Newspaper	Sad and serious

How else would you describe this story?

Cartoon	*Did not answer this question*
Poem	The dog wasn't where he shouldn't be
Play	Kind and helpful
Picture book	There are lots of animals
Diary	This story is quite upsetting
Story told in pictures	Detective
Short story	*Did not answer this question*
Newspaper	Frighening

Find your three favourite words in the piece of writing that you are looking at

Cartoon	Crash, eeek, grr
Poem	Trigger, bod, hullabaloo
Play	Funny, ooh, zoo
Picture book	Cat, frog, water
Diary	Fear, midnight, disappeared
Story told in pictures	Brilliant, proud, flash
Short story	Earthlings, earflaps, wiggly worms
Newspaper	Crew, vessel, north Cornwall coast

The children were grouped by ability while giving due consideration to group dynamics. Starting with the most able, roughly speaking, the group writing-style allocation was

- diary
- story in chapters
- short story
- cartoon
- poem
- newspaper
- play
- picture book

The questions were beyond the ability of some of the children. Much more text-focused work was needed, indicating that the introductory session was not adequate to prepare the children. They needed to look at more texts for matters such as characterisation.

This indicates that when designing such a questionnaire for your class it may be helpful to adhere to a simple set of guidelines:

- make it simple
- keep it short
- focus on no more than two themes for the children to explore at any one session
- give all the children a 'way in' to study a piece of writing; this will also provide scope to extend and challenge the most able children.

Lesson 3 – Defining character – 70 minutes

Language focus – understanding key terms: character, outline, story-board, technique, accuracy

consistency, adjectives for character descriptions

Aims
- to think about ideas for eight different sagas to be written by the eight groups
- to give the children an example of a framework which they can use to build up their own sagas

- to help the children understand the concept of drafting and redrafting

- each group to produce four character outlines for its story, i.e. each group's saga to feature four characters

Materials

- task sheet CHARACTER OUTLINE SHEET

- rough work books

Roles needed for collaborative learning in this lesson

- scribe

- reporter

Lesson

20 minutes whole class – teacher-led discussion – the children sitting in their groups

- recall what a saga is

- elicit from the children ideas about possible themes and titles for their sagas and note them on the board

- allocate different writing styles to each group, each writing style being one of the eight in which sagas will be written: diary, picture book etc

- discuss how authors draft and redraft and how on soap operas there are many writers who use story-boards and character outlines, and write copious notes

- ask the children if they have any idea why character outlines and story-boards are needed – try and elicit/suggest that this technique is needed to achieve accuracy and consistency in the character descriptions.

10 minutes group work – discussion
- the four children in each group must discuss four potential characters – what they might look like and their personalities

- one person to write these ideas down in a notebook

10 minutes whole class – feedback by the groups
- each group's reporter to tell the rest of the class his/her group's ideas of four characters

- the rest of the class to ask the reporter for more details if the children think there isn't sufficient information about the characters

- distribute CHARACTER OUTLINE SHEET to each child

- look at it together and ensure that all the children understand what they're supposed to be doing – eg. do they really understand the term outline?

10 minutes individual work – within the groups
- the group has to agree on which member writes about which character of the four that they'd agreed on at the beginning of the previous group discussion

- each child to write one character description

10 minutes whole class – feedback
- each group's reporter to read out to the class that group's four character descriptions

- the rest of the class to comment on the words used to describe the character i.e. do the adjectives fit in with the examples of the characters' behaviour?

10 minutes individual work – within groups –
- complete the character outline sheets with drawings

Evaluation of lesson three

This lesson kept everyone working purposefully and I was pleased with the children's application and the quality of their work throughout the lesson. They seemed to be constantly building on their knowledge and extending their ideas. The three completed character outline sheets, at the end of this lesson's notes, show evidence of understanding characterisation. They introduce the reader to the characters and go on to provide cohesive and appropriate details about what the characters are actually like. For example, Banana is introduced as a 'naughty, cheeky monkey' who 'plays tricks on people' and pretends that he's older that he really is. All the details link together and we, as readers, are building up a picture from the information provided.

Annie, we learn, has a good sense of humour, which leads us to believe that she might be fun to be with. In the next sentence this is confirmed – 'she likes adventures'! A human element is added to make this character believable. She is 'sometimes a pest'. There is further cohesion here too – 'she is a little bit bossy', yet 'kind' – confirmed by the fact that she tries to 'stop Yasmin chasing boys'.

Metal Stripe seems to be a 3-D character who is 'kind but mostly mean'. There is more fantasy to this character, and indeed this group's entire work (the poem group) is much occupied with fantasy, indicating that the children are formulating other issues around their character as they work.

It could be that while we are directing children's attention to one element of their saga, they are subconsciously formulating wider elements of their story. Or it could be a by-product of group discussions and negotiations. Only by tape-recording and analysing children's collaborative conversations could I have been sure of this aspect of the work. Nevertheless, if this is the case, then this has implications for using this collaborative learning approach as a stimulus in itself for future work.

All three examples of this lesson's outcome provided well-developed characters which indicate to me that the children have understood the development of characterisation as an important ingredient for a saga.

Lesson 4 – Writing and illustrating the settings for the sagas –
70 minutes
Language focus – features of writing

Aims
- to encourage the children to look at the features of various styles of writing – for example, the newspaper group look for and label features such as headlines, columns, photos and captions; the children will be given models of writings to look at – a page of a diary, a page of a newspaper and so on, on which to base their own writing

- to consider the settings for their mini sagas

Materials
Eight different examples of writing – see lesson 2, page 46.

- notebooks
- drawing paper and pencil colours/crayons
- writing paper

Roles in groups for this lesson
- scribe
- reporter
- writer
- artist/illustrator

Lesson
10 minutes whole class – teacher-led discussion
- recap on the last session – talk about characterisation, focus specifically on the requirements for developing a character; this will be linked to the idea of writing a setting

- make sure that all the children are sitting in their groups

Writing a mini saga
Character out line sheet.

Group members names

Character's name	Picture and brief description of what they are like
metal stripe	Metal stripe is mean kind as well but mostly mean. he's only kind when he feels sorry for someone he is painted black and white and has scar sticking to him, her? his always trying to find out secrets. Sometimes he might almost get killed trying to find out a secret. Especially big secrets, then he would go and tell everyone that secret he just found out. his voice was squeky he was never serious. but also cheeky. he can't read peoples minds as long as he can see them 

Writing a mini saga
Character out line sheet.

Group members names

Character's name	Picture and brief description of what they are like
Banana	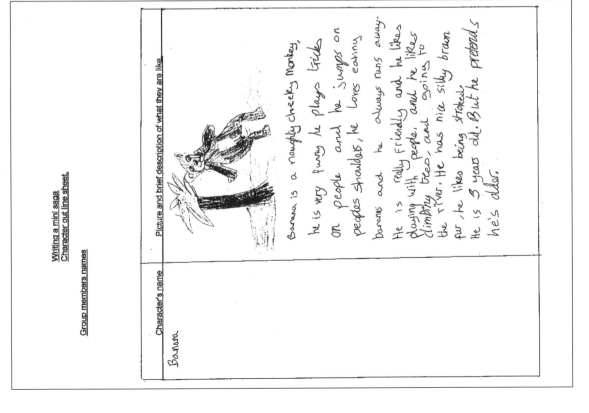 Banana is a naughty cheeky monkey. he is very funny he plays tricks on people and he jumps on peoples shoulders, he loves eating bananas and he always runs away. He is really friendly and he likes playing with people, and he likes climbing trees, and going to the river. He has nice silky brown fur, he likes being stroked. He is 5 years old. But he pretends he's older.

PHASE TWO – WRITING A MINI SAGA
EXAMPLES OF MODELS OF WRITING AND
CHILDREN'S SETTINGS

The Iron Island

There are lots of palm trees on the Iron Island. There is a river passing by the palm trees. The Iron Island has been painted so it does not look like an Iron Island. On the Iron Island there are tents. The ground is Iron sand. The tents are made from foil. Metal Stripe sleeps in the Palm trees.

Tent

The tent is gigantic, the tent is a Mess and no one has ever used their bin. The tent is white and black Stripes. Aluminium foil Sleeps in the tent. Skinny fish and fat fish Sleeps in the Sea.

Its a beautiful city.
Its in 1997.
Its in a city.
2 trees.
Near a motel.
Its near the sea.
The king lives there.
The city is 55 miles
long.
2 bowling alleys.

- give each group examples of writing in the style which they will compose their mini sagas

10 minutes group work – discuss and record
- ask each group to look at the examples together

- ask the scribes to note down as many facts as they can about that particular style of writing eg. look at the pictures, types of words, layout – and record them on a sheet

10 minutes whole class – report back and teacher-led discussion
- each group's reporter to read to the class that group's findings

- talk about the setting of a story – the setting for their stories must fit in with their ideas for the story

- emphasise that the setting should not keep changing without a link and that it should not change too many times

5 minutes group work
- discuss an appropriate setting for their particular type of writing e.g the diary group will need to consider a setting for their diary story

- move into pairs

25 minutes pair-work
- each of the two pairs in each of the groups will now consider two different settings – one per pair

- in each pair one child will write as interesting a description as possible, while the other child draws a detailed picture of the setting

10 minutes whole class – feedback
- each pair will report back – the writer will read the setting description while the artist holds up the drawing for viewing

- the class will judge the accuracy of the written description against the illustration

Evaluation of lesson 4

The poem group have linked their location to their characterisation in terms of the iron/metal theme and have successfully set the scene broadly in terms of describing the island itself and have then focused on a setting-within-a-setting – the tent.

The poem that the children looked at as a model – Dog in the Playground by Alan Ahlberg – does not set the scene in an overt way. It requires readers to draw on their own experiences of the playground and on more subtle differences throughout the poem, to create their own mental picture of the scene as the poem unfolds. Thus this group has gone further than their model poem in terms of describing the setting, which indicates that they appreciated the inferences of the setting in the model poem and that they are drawing on existing knowledge about scene-setting from other books they know. Indeed, it is interesting that they chose 'iron' as their theme as we had recently done English work about The Iron Man by Ted Hughes.

Dog In the Playground is a poem with much rhyme and repetition. The poem group's setting similarly contains a great deal of repetition of the and there at the beginning of their verses. Viewed one way, it gives a somewhat stilted and basic reading. Viewed in the context of the model poem, the repetition gives a poetical feel to the children's writing.

When we look at the settings constructed by the play and cartoon groups for their sagas, we see a similar repetitive style. The children appear to be making definite statements about the settings – that they are formulating clear pictures in their heads. Once again, these foundations provide the children and the teacher with material to develop and extend their use of language, with regard to setting, in future lessons.

The pairs worked well together. Both children in each pair had something to do and, because the writing of the poem and its illustration had to complement one another, it encouraged purposeful collaborative discussion throughout. That is, although the scribe would be solely responsible for the physical process of writing, the child drawing would have to help with ideas, and vice versa. There had to be points of convergence between the writing and the picture, and this could only be achieved by the two children bouncing ideas off each other, agreeing on a character's mental attributes and how this could be presented pictorially.

PHASE FOUR
Lesson 5 – Bring together characters and settings to create events
– 1 hour

Language focus – variety in sentence construction and breadth of vocabulary according to style

Aims

- for the groups to come up with four sequenced ideas for their mini sagas

- to use the characters and settings that they have already established

- to begin to create a word bank for their mini sagas

Materials

- 'Sequence of events' task sheet and one OHP transparency of the same

Roles needed in this session

- scribe
- reporter

Lesson

10 minutes whole class – teacher-directed discussion

- discuss the need for planning an outline for a story before writing it in detail: with a blank Sequence of Events OHP transparency elicit from the children a list of events in a well known story, Goldilocks and the three bears, i.e. in terms of events 1,2,3,4, etc; ask the children to say who is/was involved in each event and to think about why the author might choose such an approach to telling the story; expected response should be that the story needs to flow and make sense; point out that the author can add all the extra detail about characterisation and setting after the events have been decided upon

15 minutes group work – discuss and make notes

- the groups must discuss four events in their mini saga and reach an agreement
- the scribe must write down in a notebook the basic ideas of the group

15 minutes whole class – feedback by groups

- the groups' reporters to read out their groups' ideas for four sequenced events in their mini sagas
- the rest of the class must try and remember all the other groups' settings and characters as they were reported in the previous session and judge if the others are keeping a coherent line of thought
- distribute the 'Sequence of events' task sheet to every child in each group

20 minutes individual work – within groups

- each child must outline one of the events in the saga as the group has already agreed
- each child's contribution must fit to the flow of the story so that the final story reads as if it had been written by one person only
- each child must contribute uniquely to the vocabulary of the story (i.e. to the story's word bank) in such a way that the words chosen to describe the events are in line with the group's original idea for the story as a whole

Writing a saga
Sequence of events.

Event 1

Characters Involved

Aluminium foil & Metal Stripe

Setting

The Iron Island

What Happens Aluminum foil goes for a Swim in river becouse it is too hot and he Might Melt. And metal stripe Sees him from his bed in the palm tree and follows.

Event 2

Characters Involved   Aluminum foil , Metal Stipe

Setting

The Iron Island

What Happens

Then Aluminum foil Swam to the bottom following a fish when he saw Something and it was a arrow pointing north So Aluminum foil Went north.

Event 3

Characters Involved Metal stripe and Skinny fish fat fish and Aluminun foil.

Setting Iron island river.

What Happens He faund a treasure map, he follows it and finds the treasure he met Skinny fish and fat fish.

Event 4

Characters fat fish, skinny fish and Aluminun foil. metal stripe

Setting iron island

What Happens Skinny fish and fat fish saw the chest and asked if there was money inside it. Alumimun foil said "I dont know, I can't open it, it's stuck. Can you help open it?" "yes" said Skinny fish and fat fish together. They took the chest to the surface and got it open. "wow" said Alunimun foil, skinny fish and fat fish. Then they saw Metal stripe. "what do you want" said fat fish sternly because No one liked him. Then metal stripe saw a secret, it was "fat and skinny fish were rich and that they wanted the money"

Evaluation of lesson 5

The groups were required to bring together their characterisation (lesson 2) with the setting (lesson 3) and put them together into a narrative of events, all of which which would be linked to the final outcome. They worked from a task sheet sequencing four events and asking about each: Characters involved? Setting? What happens?

The poem group does this very quickly. Metal Stripe, we are told in the setting description, sleeps in palm trees. The character outline sheet informs us that he is always trying to uncover out secrets. In event one these two ideas are pulled together as Metal Stripe follows Aluminium Foil. In event four, the idea that Metal Stripe is mean is confirmed – 'no one liked him'.

The structure of the sequence of events is interesting too. The events flow well and the endings of events one, two and three are left hanging. The group had understood and remembered from lesson one's outcome that episodes end on cliff-hangers, have the same characters throughout and are interesting adventures.

By this stage the children are used to working as a group and taking on a variety of roles within it. They are successfully pulling ideas together from previous lessons to make some quite sophisticated links, as the examples show.

PHASE FIVE
Lesson 6 – Producing the eight sagas – 1 hour
Language focus – cohesive writing and adherence to the selected style

Aims
- for the children to begin bringing together their ideas for the characters, settings and events
- to begin to draft and redraft a powerful opening that fits in with the genre in which the groups are presenting their mini saga

Materials
- all preparatory work done in the previous four phases
- eight models of eight writing genres as reminder stimuli for each of the eight groups
- drawing equipment
- writing paper

Roles needed in this lesson

- three writers in each group

- one illustrator in each group

- reporter

Lesson

10 minutes whole class – preparation
- make sure that all children are sitting in their genre groups and that they have all work done so far on their desks

- tell them that they are going to remind themselves of the genre each group will be writing in

- distribute writing genre stimuli sheets to each group – eg. press article to newspaper group and so on

10 minutes group work – discussion
- read together the genre models in which they are going to write

- discuss its properties, especially how the genre opens the story

- relate back to the work already done on style and check that they've not left anything out of their previous consideration

- if it will help them, jot down a checklist of key elements to their particular style

10 minutes whole class – report back
each group's reporter to give the rest of the class a quick recap of what that group will be writing about and in what style

30 minutes group work – writing and illustrating the saga
- two of the four children in each group to start drafting the opening of the story

- one child to use the notes from their previous preparatory work to write a blurb which will appear at the back of the cover of the saga just as published books have blurbs on the back cover

- the fourth child to start on the illustrations, also referring to all previous notes.

COMMENTS ON THE COMPLETION OF THE SAGAS

When writing up the sagas the children were required to be very organised about using existing information and reproducing it in their allocated genre. The poem group had apparently managed to tie together all these elements as well as rhythm and structure. This, I feel, reflects improving use of language in both their oral and their written work. Unfortunately their written work does not reflect the richness of their discussions, in which they confidently used terms like characterisation, saga, cliff-hangers, sequence of events.

The children settled more quickly into their groups and were more aware of their own roles and the roles of their peers in the group. The members of the group had matured towards interdependence and were not timid about seeking and offering assistance, making suggestions and improvements. Disagreements still arose but these became easier to deal with. Collaborative learning had equipped the children with some of the skills to solve conflict: greater tolerance, more listening, greater respect, reaching a compromise.

The final product – the saga – shows evidence of having brought together all the ingredients of the previous lessons, demonstrating the value of the sequential way that the writing project had been designed. The children had used these lessons as the foundations of an experience from which to build and develop in terms of collaborative skills and language development.

An example of this is the poetry group. A, a bilingual pupil, initially found the style of poetry writing difficult to appreciate, but with the collaborative efforts of the other children in this group – and with the help of the model text – he became more aware of the genre of English his group was studying. He gradually gained a better understanding of poetry and with his increasing comprehension came greater confidence in his own contributions to the group's work. This group was of average academic ability. Socially they were not in each other's peer groups. Yet they learnt to work well collaboratively to produce some good language work. Social and academic development can complement each other.

The time taken to finish the stories varied considerably between the groups. The advantage of collaborative work is that by this stage the children are aware of their roles. The ground-work has been done and the children are fairly independent and enthusiastic to complete the work. So it's relatively easy at the final stage to fit in the finishing work into any odd moments during the day.

When the mini sagas were complete, they were bound into individual books to be shared by the whole class.

THE POETRY GROUP'S MINI SAGA

THE IRON ISLAND

One sunny day
The boss of the Iron island
Aluminium Foil, greedy, funny, sometimes bossy
That's Aluminium Foil,
Went for a swim
In the blue, blue river

And Metal Stripe,
An iron painted badger
Saw him from his bed
High up, in the highest palm
Tree.

Metal Stripe is usually mean,
He loves to sift out secrets
Especially the BIG secrets
And then he tells every one else,
In his squeaky voice.

Aluminium Foil saw a big gold fish
Swimming in the river
He started to follow the fish
It went to the bottom of the river.

Aluminium Foil found
An arrow end pointed to the surface
He followed it..........................
And to his surprise
It led him to a treasure map.

He swam through the river,
He followed the map
Around the metal trees
Finally he shouted
YESSS! He shouted in
Amazement.

He jumped up and he
Opened the box and found a gold crown.
He looked around when he heard a sound
Fat fish then skinny fish then popped up
Aluminium Foil jumped out of his skin.
As he saw skinny fish and fat fish.

They asked 'Is there any money?'
'It's stuck' Aluminium shouted.
'I can't open it'.
'Can you help open it?'
'YES' shouted Skinny Fish and Fat Fish together
Let's take it to the surface and open it' said Fat Fish.
'YES' shouted Aluminium.

So they took it to the surface.
And opened it. 'WOW' all of them said.
'Look at that TREASURE' said Skinny Fish.
'And all that gold' said Aluminium Foil
Metal Stripe came and Fat fish turned and saw him.

'What do you want?' said Fat Fish.
'Let's give him some money' said Aluminium Foil.
'No one likes him'.
'Alright then' Skinny Fish so they all
Had a happy time and they all bought
Paint for their clothes.

The iron Island

An excting adventure about 4
Iron people living on an island finding
treasure and finding out mysterious
secrets. A normal river look's like
any other river but is not, look
in side and see for me, you
Might find some secrets!!

Concluding thoughts

'Did it go well?' and 'Would you do it again?' are questions that I imagine teachers ask their colleagues about innovative lessons.

The mini saga project is very demanding. A great deal is required in terms of organisation, management, preparation and planning. But once the project is underway it tends to run by itself as the children become more independent. I am writing these reflective remarks with faded memories of initial problems in terms of group dynamics – arguments, power struggles and refusal to co-operate with others (does this sound familiar?). Nevertheless, I feel that the problems are in some way the justification for doing the project. The children had to work through the problems and learn to work with others. It contributes to their social development.

A striking outcome of this project was the language development of the children, evident throughout the work. Yet in a way, the final product was just a small part of the work – it is all too easy to forget all the discussion and collaboration that goes into such activities.

In terms of linguistic development, this on-going project allowed children to improve their vocabulary and grammar, for example, how to use vocabulary appropriately to describe characters and settings. The children's technical use of vocabulary improved with their awareness of styles and structure of various writing genres. This was reflected not only in their own writing but also in discussions within and outside the groups. They became more competent at identifying features of a saga, such as cliff-hangers, and the development of the story lines.

So if you want to examine a genre of writing in depth and would like your class to work in harmony, some of these ideas may be worth trying. It is a productive and refreshing way for the class and the teacher to focus on literacy by studying texts, with discussion as a basis for the development of writing.

GRAMMAR WORK WITH YEAR 4 CLASS 1997-1998
VERBS AND COLLABORATIVE LEARNING

NATIONAL CURRICULUM – DEF, 1995, p 16

NATIONAL LITERACY HOUR – DfEE, 1998, p 42

THE CLASSROOM: 30 pupils

Average ability level – between levels 3 and 4 in English

General delivery of curriculum: subject based and whole class; provision for individual, pair and group work

Generally the groups were selected on the basis of mixed ability. The children worked and co-operated well. They were enthusiastic, interested and well motivated. Yet in class discussions it would always be the same few who participated willingly. Though others would have opinions of their own or know the answers to questions, they would be reticent and possibly fearful of being wrong. This is why I decided to approach this work on the verb with this class on a collaborative learning basis. I wanted to provide definite reasons and opportunities for *all* children to volunteer their thinking and reasoning in pairs, groups and class discussions.

This was a three-session programme in which I wanted the children to become aware that

- verbs are essential grammatical components to making and communicating accurate meaning

- the concept of the past – of what has been and gone – is expressed with the same verbs that express the same thought/event/state-of-being in the present, the here-and-now

- these verbs require a different spelling for the past and the present

- there are regular and irregular verbs and this affects the past tense spelling

- the spelling of some regular verbs in the past may not follow the simple rule of other regular verbs

- when we choose to use a particular verb in a sentence we do so to make our meaning clear

- verbs are fun words which we can manipulate.

One important consideration in the learning of grammar is how to present it to children of this age group – how much to tell the children and how much to let them deduce for themselves. I did not want to stand in front of the class, point to some words in a sentence and utter ominous words like 'this is a verb' and 'this is a verb in the past tense'! On the other hand, the children need to learn to use the appropriate terminology with which to look at language more critically. For example, it's no good talking about the doing words in the poem that we studied in this programme because not all the verbs are doing words! Whereas the term verb actually covers all the different types of verbs used in the poem by the poet.

So the collaborative approach to learning is a perfect way for children to:

- investigate grammar

- look for grammatical rules

- formulate grammatical rules

- study grammar in authentic text

- appreciate why, if we change the grammar of a sentence in a text, or a verb in a poem, we change the whole essence of its original meaning.

VERBS AND COLLABORATIVE LEARNING
Session One – Identify verbs and the past tense – 50 minutes

Aims – for the children

- to identify and define verbs

- to identify the present and past tense of regular verbs

- to work with a partner

- to encourage the children to identify patterns in regular verbs

- to guide the children towards inducing the grammatical rule for constructing the past tense of regular verbs

Challenge

- to use the sentences (A) to identify verbs in the present tense and put them in the past tense

- to work in pairs to create a sentence with a verb in the present tense

Materials and resources

- a list of sentences (the number is arbitrary) on a transparency – Sentences A

- an overhead projector (this is not mandatory! A large sheet or the board will do perfectly)

- strips of paper, each one with two sentences from list A

The sentences can be taken from texts that the children have looked at or made up to match the class's interests. The verbs must be regular.

Pace of lesson

5 minutes whole class – teacher-directed class discussion
*   Put the sentences transparency on the OHP and encourage the children to identify verbs

*   Ask questions such as 'What's happening?' and 'How can we tell? Which words tell us what's happening?'

3 minutes pair work –
*   give each pair of children a strip of paper with two sentences from the OHP list

*   ask the children to underline the word that tells you what happened in each sentence

5 minutes whole class – teacher-directed discussion
*   ask children to come to the front of the class one at a time, and underline the doing word on one of the OHP sentences

*   ask the rest of the children to agree or disagree with their classmate's choice

*   elicit from the class that these underlined words are verbs: eg. what did he do to the ball? point to do and ask: what type of a word is this? What information does it give us? Elicit that the verbs give us information on what the team did

5 minutes pair-work –
*   ask the children to write two sentences of their own on the back of the strips of paper they already have

*   each of these two sentences must contain a verb 'as if it is happening now'

10 minutes whole class – children's feedback
*   invite four children from four pairs to feed back to the class by reading their pair's sentences out aloud

*   instruct the rest of the class to listen carefully and check two things: that the sentences been written as if the event is happening now and that the pairs have identified the verb correctly

10 minutes whole class – teacher-led discussion
*   children go back and ask the whole class to listen

*   introduce the term present tense to the class and say that it can be used instead of 'happening now' – link it to 'being present' when answering the register in the morning

- elicit the past from the class by asking them what we might say if something had happened already: ask questions of what the children did, eg. what did you do at playtime? Expected answer may be 'I played football'

- go back to OHP sentences and ask children what they think needs to be added to the verbs in the sentences to put them in the past tense

- write on the OHP with a different colour pen by adding the appropriate ending to the verbs (-ed, -ped, etc) to the verbs as the children verbally change them one by one

2 minutes pair-work
- ask the children to change the verb in the two sentences they wrote into the past tense

10 minutes whole class – children's feedback and rule deduction
- ask one child from each pair to read out the pair's sentences

- stop after each sentence to consider the verb and its past tense spelling

- questions to consider: why does a verb like score just add a d? why does a verb like skip have an extra p before adding ed? but jump also ends in a p, so why doesn't it too have an extra p?

- Guide the children to discover the rule (if there is a vowel before the p you must add an extra p, etcetera)

SENTENCES A (OHP)

They start the football

He kicks the ball

He scores a goal

He shouts 'Hooray'

He skips around the football pitch

The team jumps for joy

The team lifts the trophy up into the air

The crowd cheers with joy

The children jump up and down

The pop group plays their song

The people listen to the music

The audience claps at the end of the song

I type a letter to my friend

The children cycle to school

- Recap by asking the children to:

  - define a verb

  - verbalise the difference in spelling of the verbs in present and past tense

  - recall that the rules just found refer only to regular verbs in the past tense

End of session

Collect the slips of paper on which the children wrote their own present tense sentences and choose a few that contain regular verbs. Later on, in IT time, one child will type these sentences and the list will be given on a sheet of paper for homework. The instructions are that they must underline the verb in the sentence and then turn the verb into the past tense. Sheet B contains these sentences and next to it is an example of a child's completion of this task.

Evaluation of session one

The time limits helped maintain the interest and enthusiasm of the children for the entire lesson. The fact that they worked in pairs on a directed activity provided a reason to work collaboratively – i.e. they would quickly see an end result. It also gave some children greater confidence to report back to the class: they had already bounced ideas off their partners. By having clearly defined aims and by making these known to the children, I had developed their knowledge and understanding of verbs by the end of the session.

HOMEWORK SENTENCES B

(created by the children)

Verbs

Underline the verb in each sentence
Put the verb into the past tense above each one

The girl plays with her doll

The lawyer yells 'no'

I jog a mile or two

I play tennis with my friend

I climb up the wall

They start the football match

The boy looks pale

The children wait for their friends

HOMEWORK SHEETS B

Verbs

Underline the verb in each sentence.
Put the verb into the past tense above each one.

played
The girl plays with her doll.

yelled
The lawyer yells, "no."

jogged
I jog a mile or two.

played
I play tennis with my friend.

climbed
I climb up the wall.

started
They start the football match.

looked
The boy looks pale.

waited
The children wait for their friends.

Session Two – Meanings and verbs – 50 minutes

Aims – for the children

*   to use existing knowledge and understanding of verbs when looking at a poem

*   to work collaboratively both in pairs and in groups of four

*   to demonstrate their understanding of the verbs' definitions in the poem by substituting them with their own verbs (cf. National Curriculum require-ment for KS2 English, pages 15 and 16, and the National Literacy Hour requirements for Year 4, term 3, page 43)

Challenge

*   To discuss the poem 'A hot day' as a class and identify the verbs in it

*   To work with a partner to substitute the verbs from a section of the poem with verbs of their own choice

Materials and resources

*   A copy and a transparency of the poem 'A hot day' by A. S. J. Tessimond (taken from the New Nelson handwriting copy-master book)

*   Overhead projector (OHP)

*   Cut up strips of the poem, each strip containing exactly one third of the poem and its verbs removed for pair and group work – see below

*   One A4 sheet with two printouts of the poem – one original version and one with blank spaces from where the verbs have been removed

Pace of the lesson

15 minutes whole class – teacher-directed discussion

*   read the poem to the class

*   ask individual children (maximum six) for any words they like or dislike in the poem they've just heard

*   offer my own choice of likes or dislikes – which will be verbs

*   give reasons to the children for my own likes and dislikes, eg. I like 'weaves' because it describes beautifully what the sunlight does with the leaves and gives the poem some rhyme and rhythm

*   ask the children if they can tell the teacher what sort of words the teacher likes or dislikes – eliciting the term verb

- can the children say what these words – chosen by the teacher – are doing in their particular place in the poem?

- identify all the verbs verbally

- put poem transparency on the OHP and ask the children to read out the verbs

- underline all the verbs on the OHP and discuss the meaning of them as we go along

10 minutes pair-work – the poem has been divided into three sections
- give each pair a copy of a section of the poem with the verbs blanked out – Task sheet one

- tell the children that the class of thirty has been divided into three groups of ten each, each having five pairs working on one third of the poem

- ask the children to fill the gaps in their section of the poem with any verb they want

5 minutes group work – four children in each group
- put each set of partners with another set who are working on the same section of the poem

- allocate four roles to this newly formed group: chairperson, writer, spell-checker and a child to report back to the class on the group's choice of verbs and the reasons why each verb was selected

- tell them to feed back their work to one another and to decide on a final verb for each blank space in their section of the poem

20 minutes whole class – teacher-led discussion
- each group reporter to read out to the rest of the class the verbs selected by the group to replace the original verbs in their section of the poem and justify the selected verbs

- as a class, discuss the alternative selection of verbs by the seven groups and decide on a final class selection – 4m's version of the poem is given below

- write in the class selection of verbs on a full copy of the poem with all its original verbs taken out: one sheet per child plus a copy on the OHP

End of session – Set homework

At the end of the day, after copying the class's version alongside the original version of the poem, give the children each a sheet with both these versions on and tell them to read them again at home and write underneath one sentence for each of five verbs. Any of the five verbs can be chosen from either the original version or the class's version. They must say which verbs they prefer and why. An example of the children's homework task sheet is given at the end of this lesson's notes.

Assessment of the children's work

The children were slow to come up with the term verb (see first 15 minutes of class discussion), but eventually they managed it. They could identify that some of the words I liked were 'doing words', or added a certain style to the poem, but it took a while to elicit the term verb. This demonstrates the problem of trying to get the children to guess what the teacher wants. They need fairly tight guidelines to work within but at the same time they need breadth, so they can fully explore and express their reactions to the poem or any other text.

However, the verbs selected by the children were appropriate to my aims of this three-session programme, in so far as they communicated accurate meanings. The verbs were all in the present tense and, importantly, the children enjoyed experimenting with verbs in a way that moved quickly towards an end result.

The children were focused on their tasks. They were aware of what was required of them in each set amount of time and responded well.

Although I've set out a series of lessons on verbs, I have also used exactly the same approach with other aspects of language work such as adjectives with pleasing success. The combinations of language work within this basic format are numerous and can easily be adapted to meet your own requirements.

Preview of follow-up work

The children will work collaboratively to produce a similar poem of their own.

Observations on the children's choice of alternative verbs

The children and I were pleased with the alternative verbs and the way they fitted into the existing poem. Having the poem as a framework to work with had focused them on the quality, meaning and effect of the verbs. An additional benefit was that they became absorbed in the poem itself. They were quite aware that although some of their alternative verbs had similar meanings to the original ones, they could change the overall effect of the poem.

Page 80 shows how the children worked. In the pair work session, when each pair had one third of the poem, pairs had to come up with alternative verbs that would fit the climate of the whole poem as well as the third allocated to the pairs. Each group then had to make a definitive selection of the verb from two different verbs (initially selected by the pairs) and give their reasons for this selection. The children's comments on how the groups arrived at their final choice are significant: 'everybody agreed' – section one; 'we voted for them' – section two. What splendid examples of democratic collaboration!

This work highlights learning on two levels. Firstly the language – the children commented on the verbs as words that 'made sense' and were 'good words'.

A Hot Day

Cottonwool clouds loiter
A lawnmower, very far,
Birrs. Then a bee comes
To a crimson rose and softly,
Deftly and fatly crams
A velvet body in.

A tree, June-lazy, makes
A tent of dim green light.
Sunlight weaves in the leaves,±
Honey-light laced with leaf-light,
Green interleaved with gold.
Sunlight gathers its rays
In sheaves, which the wind unweaves
And then reweaves – the wind
That puffs a smell of grass
Through the heat-heavy, trembling
Summer pool of air.

A. S. J. Tessimond

EXAMPLES OF ALTERNATIVE VERBS SUGGESTED BY ONE PAIR

Cottonwool clouds **hover**
A lawnmower, very far,
Spatters. *Then a bee* **passes**
To a crimson rose and softly
Deftly and fatly **squeezes**
A velvet body in.

A tree, June-lazy, **builds**
A tent of dim green light.
Sunlight **blows** *in the leaves.*
Honey-light **swims** *with leaf-light,*
Green **shines** *with gold*

Sunlight **moves** *its rays*
In sheaves, which the wind **calms**
And then **unweaves** *– the wind*
That **makes** *a smell of grass*
Through the heat-heavy, **shaking**
Summer pool of air

THREE GROUPS' CHOSEN VERBS AND THE REASONS GIVEN

We choose these words: drift, skims, hovers, squeezes and unravelled because they made sense and there were good words to put and everybody agreed to choose these certain words.

A Hot Day ~~drift~~

Cottonwool clouds _Float_

A lawnmower, very far,

~~Skims~~. Then a bee _hovers_

To a crimson rose and softly,

Deftly and fatly _Squeezes_

A velvet body in.

We chose these verbs because we voted for them,
One person said a verb and the rest voted.

A tree, June-lazy, _stands_

A tent of dim green light.

Sunlight _Glimes_ in the leaves,

Honey-light _yellow_ with leaf-light.

Green _leaves_ with gold.

We chose collects because it was a bit simpler than moves.
We chose unweaves because everyone agreed.
We chose blows because it makes sense.
We chose shaking because that was the only one we knew.

Sunlight **collects** its rays

In sheaves. which the wind

And then **unweaves** the wind

That **blows** the smell of grass

Through the heat-heavy. **Shaking**

Summer pool of air.

A Hot Day

Class 4m's final version of the poem with alternative verbs selected after pairs of children and then groups of four had deliberated on a variety of possibilities

Cottonwool clouds **drift**
A lawnmower, very far,
Skims. *Then a bee* **hovers**
To a crimson rose and softly,
Deftly and fatly **squeezes**
A velvet body in.

A tree, June-lazy, **creates**
A tent of dim green light.
Sunlight **glimmers** *in the leaves,*
Honey-light **weaves** *with leaf-light,*
Green **shines** *with gold.*
Sunlight **collects** *its rays*
In sheaves, which the wind **unravels**
And then **unwinds** *– the wind*
That **blows** *a smell of grass*
Through the heat-heavy, **shaking**
Summer pool of air.

They focused on verbs as grammatical units in the sentence which gave meanings to the poet's ideas. At the same time they were evaluating the verbs' quality and suitability within the wider text of the poem. Secondly, social skills – working fairly, negotiating and collaborating on something with a purpose and an end result. The groups worked hard and collaborated really well. To work hard in the selection of verbs for the poem and then possibly not ultimately use them requires a skilful use of debate, persuasion and compromise, as well as graceful surrender to the group's wishes.

Comments on the children's choice of verbs

The children used their understanding and appreciation of the poem to select verbs that they felt matched the original ones and maintained the flow and feel of the poem. Within a short time they had unconsciously gained quite a sophisticated appreciation of the poem.

When the children had realised that the words I initially highlighted were verbs, they could quickly identify the other verbs in the poem. By directing the children to focus on one key element of the poem in their discussion, i.e. the verb, they were able to broaden their observations to the context and imagery of the poem. Concentrating on one linguistic element of the poem at the beginning of such language possibly provides a sort of foothold from which to examine the rest of the poem. Success in identifying and commenting on the verbs will have given the children the confidence and knowledge to examine other aspects of the poem.

We were halfway through this programme of three lessons on the verb and I wanted the children to transfer some of their learning from lesson one. I am satisfied that the children did so and built on it in this second lesson. Their discussions indicated a livelier and more confident use of appropriate grammatical terminology and their written work shows interesting usage of the verbs. I also wanted this work to be carried through into session three, when children would be required to demonstrate their understanding of verbs as meaningful items of language to make sense of their own poems.

Session 3 – Verbs in creative writing – 2hrs 15mins

Aims

- to continue to develop children's collaborative skills

- to extend the children's use of verbs in their own writing

- to draw on the children's other grammatical knowledge – nouns – to make the link between nouns and verbs

- to use the poem 'A Hot Day' as a model for children's own work

Challenge

To write a poem called 'On A Hot Day' in collaboration with other class members, paying specific attention to verbs. The poem should have four verses, each concentrating on smell, touch, sight or hearing. The children were to work in the following sequence: individually, then in pairs, and finally in groups of four

Materials

- poem 'A Hot Day' (see page 77) on an OHP transparency as stimulus for the class discussion at the start of the lesson

- grid sheets for sensory work outside in the school playground. Susan, what did grid sheet look like? Can you redraw it?

- paper for jotting down work at each stage

- large sheets on which to stick the verses of the poem

Pace of lesson – these are the times spent on each task:

15 minutes whole class – teacher-led discussion
- recap on the poem 'A Hot Day' used in session two

- read it through and discuss the nouns and verbs and how they link to the senses of sight, smell, hearing and touch

- ask the children to select verbs from the poem and relate them to the appropriate senses, eg. 'what does the verb weaves make you think of? Seeing, hearing, touching or smelling?'

- tell the children that they are going to go outside into the fields to produce a similar poem together

- instruct the children to pay close attention to what they can hear, see, smell and touch and think of outside – and to jot down nouns on the prepared sheet under the appropriate headings – nouns and verbs that link to what they can see, hear, smell and touch

10 minutes individual work – outside
- all the children to jot down words for sight, hearing, smell and touch on their grid sheets

10 minutes group work – back in the classroom
- the children return to their groups and number each child one, two, three, and four

- tell them that each child is responsible for collating the group's suggestions for a particular sense as they had jotted down in the playground, one on sight, one on hearing, one on smell and the fourth on touch.

15 minutes pair work –
- split the groups of four and re-organise the children to work with a partner from a different group who has the same number

- eg. Group A Group B   Group C Group D

    child 1<<<<<>>>child 1   child 1<<<<<>>>child 1

    child 2<<<<<>>>child 2   child 2<<<<<>>>child 2

    child 3<<<<<>>>child 3   child 3<<<<<>>>child 3

    child 4<<<<<>>>child 4   child 4<<<<<>>>child 4

- members of each new partnership share their original group's work: i.e. child one from group A and child one in group B exchange ideas about their collated lists on sight from each other's group

- tell these new pairs of children to select two verbs each that they think could best be used in a verse of a poem; for example children 2 from each group selected four verbs on hearing

- eg. children with number 1 from groups A and B share their group's information on sight and select four verbs to be used for their verse about the things they saw 'On A Hot Day' – which will be the title of their own poem

10 minutes whole class – feedback

some children from different pairs will explain their choice of verbs and the reasons for choosing them – it will not be possible to go through the whole class, so six pairs at most will be asked to report back

15 minutes pair-work

- ask the children to work together to put together one verse for the poem

- the verse must contain their chosen verbs

- the poem must be about their chosen sense

- the poem must be written in a style similar to the original by Tessimond

10 minutes group work

- the children are to return to their original groups of four

- starting with child number 1, each is to read out the verse written by all the number 1 children in the last session, and so on until a poem of four verses materialises from the readings

- the children must now think about the flow of the poem – do they think that one verse flows well into the next?

- encourage them to make any changes that they feel would improve the poem as a whole

10 minutes individual work – within each group

- having put the poem together, encourage the children to make any alterations that will improve the flow of the poem; each child to write one verse with own alterations

15 minutes group work

- each group reassembles

- each group arranges all four verses on a large sheet of paper to create the group's poem

- the poem will be illustrated later by each member of the group

15 minutes whole class – round up

- ask each group to read out the poem to the class, with each child reading the verse she/he wrote

- the rest of the class listen carefully to pick out a well used verb from each poem

Two of the poems are reproduced opposite and overleaf.

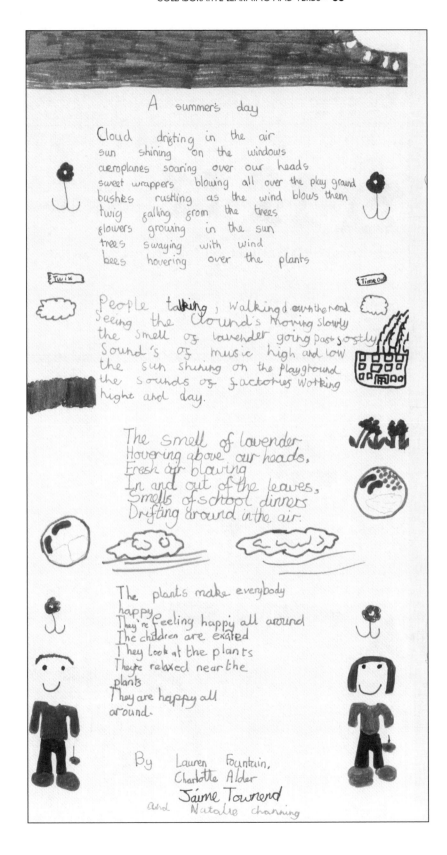

A summer's day

Cloud drifting in the air
sun shining on the windows
aeroplanes soaring over our heads
sweet wrappers blowing all over the play ground
bushes rustling as the wind blows them
twig falling from the trees
flowers growing in the sun
trees swaying with wind
bees hovering over the plants

People talking, Walking down the road
Seeing the Clound's moving slowly
the smell of lavender going past softly
Sound's of music high and low
the sun shining on the playground
the sounds of factories working
night and day.

The smell of lavender
Hovering above our heads,
Fresh air blowing
In and out of the leaves,
Smells of school dinners
Drifting around in the air.

The plants make everybody
happy
They're feeling happy all around
The children are exsited
They look at the plants
They're relaxed near the
plants
They are happy all
around.

By Lauren Fountain,
Charlotte Alder
Jaime Townend
and Natalie channing

One Summers day
The trees are swaying
Miss Moule is walking past the tree
Children playing in the playground
Clouds drifting to the air
the birds are singing in the tree
bushes are waving in the wind

A plane floats through the air
Gliding like a eagle in the air
Hearing dogs barking loudly
Cats purring, washing themselves too.
People walking through the streets
Car rumbling as he passes by
Lavender patches smells sweet (Just a little
Bit)
Grounds bumpy with pebbles scattered
Everywhere
Miss Moule walking, everbody talking, Children
writing, Trees swaying.

The lovely smell of school dinners in Summer.
Polluting smell of fumes.
Sweet perfume of lavender.
The strong whiff of bushes and trees floating to
my nose.
The fresh smell of some air.
Flowers, bushes, Trees, Grass and plants all smell
beautiful.

The warm day makes me feel ha
The sun is shining gold
The birds are singing in the trees
The light shimmers on the leaves
The sweet smell of flowers
The children playing in the playground
The trees swaying side to side
The day is calm

The children's poems

These two examples are representative of those produced. It is worth making two comments about them and their wider implications for many classrooms.

1. The way verbs are used by the children is telling, and points the way to future work that would need to be done on the verbs. In both poems there is much use of the verbs in the –ing form, either as part of the present continuous tense (as in 'the trees are swaying', line two, Poem One) or as an adjective which lends dramatic effect to the intended imagery (verse two, Poem Two).

Poem One uses fifteen different verbs – mostly ending in –ing, and twenty –ing expressions in all. Poem Two has twenty-four different verbs – of which twenty end in –ing. The two poems together have four present tenses (actually seven, but one verb – 'they are' – is repeated three times in section four) and one past participle ('scattered').

If we look again at the poem the children studied, we find that Tessimond uses the present tense more than any other. There are fifteen different verbs in 'A Hot Day', eight of which are present tense, all in the third person singular, two past participles ('laced' and 'interlaced') and one only ending in –ing ('trembling').

In these lessons we did not focus on the effect of using the present tense, as Tessimond does, compared with other verb forms. The aim was simply to look at choice of verbs, for semantic effect. However, the children's own use of verbs made me realise that they need to be directed more closely than I had realised towards the study of verbs and how we use them in their different forms to create meanings.

Why did the children employ so many –ing forms of the verbs? It could be that children are generally exposed to rhyme and rhythm from an early age – but only in a limited way. In any event, this suggests that the next step needed to be analysing the different tenses and how these are used in poems or stories, to see what effect and impact choice of tense has on the reader.

2. The last verses of Poems One and Two – the sections on feelings – did not fulfil the aims of the lesson, which was for the children to find verbs for the sense of touch. Instead they produced a verse on a state of being. For example:

Poem One: 'the day makes me feel happy'
              [followed by features of the day conducive to this happy
              feeling]
              'The day is calm'

Poem Two: 'The plants make everybody happy

              ....

              ....

....

> They're relaxed near the plants
> They are happy all around'

The problem, I realise, lies in the English verb to feel which can mean: to feel the surface of something by contact eg. the grass feels damp under my feet, but can also mean: to feel with one's mind and/or body eg. I feel apprehensive... I feel delicate. Verbs expressing feeling in the sense of touch might be: to stroke, as in 'a butterfly flies past me and strokes my hair with its wings', or to run one's fingers through, as in 'I ran my fingers through the leaves'

It had not occurred to me that the children might confuse the two meanings, so I had not dwelt on it. It escaped my attention until the children were reading out their final version to the class in their reporting back session. They had worked very hard and were, quite rightly, excited about their poems. But I made a mental note.

One cannot take for granted that children understand the words they use, or the words we teachers use, in all the breadth of their meanings.

Observations and evaluation of these lessons on the verb

Having studied the style of the poem 'A Hot Day' in session two, the children seemed to approach with confidence the third session in which they were to try and emulate the poem's original style while changing its verbs. This procedure avoided the problems that arise when children try to guess what the teacher wants. They had already studied the qualities, functions and definitions of verbs in session one. Taking the children outside encouraged them to use their senses and draw inspiration from their surroundings.

Breaking of each lesson helped to maintain concentration. The children knew they had tight deadlines to work to. It also helped to demonstrate the various stages involved in writing a poem and working collaboratively – from jotting down ideas and brainstorming verbs to developing, refining, drafting and re-drafting and producing the final work. All the children had an equal input and responsibility to collaborate and produce a verse for their group's poem.

The two hours and fifteen minutes devoted to this work could be divided in various ways, according to time and curriculum. It could be one morning's work, with one session before and after break, say, or one hour one day followed by one and a quarter the next.

The children responded favourably and enthusiastically. They acquired further skills, knowledge and understanding of grammar under the dual umbrella of studying a text and working collaboratively. I think this approach suits a wide range of abilities. The less able did not feel threatened by out-of-context grammar-practice exercises that children are often asked to work through and there was no ceiling of attainment for any of the children. They enjoyed the challenge, as I did, of working together in refining and developing their ideas.

CONCLUSION

The importance of collaborative learning

Working as part of a team with people who have different interests, abilities and strengths can be a challenge for people of all ages. Yet throughout our lives – at school, socially and at work – we will continually be required to work with others to reach a common goal. Overcoming obstacles on the way is difficult, but working collaboratively is ultimately stimulating, enjoyable and rewarding for all involved.

When embarking on a short or long term project which will involve children working in groups, many teachers may feel at first that certain children in the class simply cannot work together. But this actually highlights the need for collaborative work, which is, moreover, a skill just like reading or writing, that needs to be taught. Children may have no idea what is involved in working with each other.

Collaborative learning is a valuable skill in its own right. Throughout the whole process learning occurs at many levels, and intellectually – through discussions about how to overcome problems and improve work – as well as socially – by providing opportunities for children of all abilities to have a valued input into their group's work and learning.

Additionally, collaborative learning can be a vehicle for learning across the curriculum. The writing project in this book concentrates on English but the flexibility of collaborative learning is such that it can be applied to all subjects. Its flexibility is demonstrated here in the examples of long term and short term projects.

Planning for collaborative learning

It is probably quite easy to see places in your long term plans where collaborative tasks would enhance learning. Once these have been identified, the next stage is to plan into your work ways of teaching the skills of collaboration.

I found it useful to give children specific tasks and roles within the work set. Roles could include a scribe, a spell-checker, an illustrator, a child to report back and a chairperson who would monitor noise, ensure turn-taking and so on. If the project is ongoing, try to rotate the roles so that all children experience a variety of challenges.

Build up the amount of collaborative work as the children become more skilled at it. At first ask the children to work in pairs on a short task on which they report back to another pair. This will focus the children on taking turns and increase their confidence to report back to larger groups.

Within each session, break the lesson into very specific chunks of time where the children have to reach clearly defined targets. Allow time between moving onto the next target for a member from each group to feed back their progress to the rest of the class. By having strict time limits to achieve small targets, the children will learn this way of organising their work and learning. They become more independent because they are more aware of what is expected of them. The teacher is freed from the more trivial questions, so can spend more time with each group discussing, challenging and extending their work.

Over the course of a few sessions, working collaboratively, the quality of discussions improve as the children learn to work together to solve problems. Having a specific role in their group makes children more aware of the importance and value of their input into the group, and this has positive implications for their self-esteem and independence.

Implications for collaborative work of the two projects described in this chapter

- Group dynamics – start collaborative learning with a few short term ideas with which you can try out different groupings to see which work best for the children and the project. If you embark on a long term project immediately it is harder to swap the groups around.

- Consider the work you expect the children to do and have plenty of examples and models of writing you require them to understand. Do not assume, for example, that children are aware of styles of newspaper reports, diaries, poems and so on. Set tasks which will focus the children on the style, language and grammar of the genre.

- As with any lesson, make your aims of collaboration clear to the children – they need a model to follow just as they need a text to look at when studying English.

- Successful collaborative learning is rewarding for both teachers and children. There are many variations on groupings – socially and academically. Select the one in which children of all abilities can have equal access to the curriculum to foster the children's self-esteem, confidence and independence.

- Through careful organisation and classroom management of collaborative learning, the teacher is able to spend more quality time with individuals and groups to develop and extend learning and meet individual needs.

- Planning Check-List
  - Classroom layout – are the tables/desks grouped to correspond to your planned collaborative activities?

  - Resources – Overhead Projector (practice its position in the classroom before you use it in front of the class) or board (can all the children see it properly?); enough copies of text to be studied so that there is no distraction because of sharing of paper, dictionaries, etc. It is important that all the resources you need are organised and in place before the children come into the classroom.

  - Timing – be sure how long you want to spend on each part of the lesson and make sure that the children know too.

  - Group dynamics – consider what you want the children to achieve socially and academically and group them accordingly.

CHAPTER 3
THE FUTURE TENSE IN THE NATIONAL LITERACY HOUR

Keith Peterson

Fleetville JM School, St. Albans, Hertfordshire

THE SCHOOL

Fleetville JM is a large maintained county junior school for girls and boys aged 7-11. Children come from both single and dual parent families and a significant number are from ethnic minority backgrounds, which the school recognises as a strength. Children generally transfer from Fleetville Infants at 7 years of age. The school currently has 21.3% of its pupils on the SEN Register.

The school is housed in a one and two storey building to which a wing was added in the 1950s. It originally housed a girls' secondary school, becoming Fleetville JM in 1975. The space thus accorded is a genuine factor in the potential extension of learning opportunities.

Fleetville currently has 289 children on roll and the headteacher and governing body have taken the decision to expand to three forms of entry with numbers in the region of 325 by September 2000.

PANDA report information

[Performance and Assessment Information – sent to all schools yearly by the Department for Education and Employment]

- the percentage of pupils eligible for free school meals – 7% – is below the national average

- the percentage of pupils speaking English as an additional language – 9.1% – is high

- the percentage of pupils identified as having special needs – 21.3% – is in line with the national average

- the attendance rate during the 1996/97 academic year was above the national average.

Attainment at age 11: English Orders

Tests: %
Level 4 or above – 91%
Level 5 or above – 34%

The OFSTED: report of September 1998 observed that 'Pupils achieve very high standards in English' and that 'The school has developed good strategies for literacy'.

The school's values are :

- that each child be equally afforded value and respect and an entitlement to achievement

- that each child be encouraged to grow in self-esteem and positive independence

- that the school be recognised and esteemed as a community – with a parallel emphasis on communal care and responsibility

- that integral school improvement is best effected through quality of communication and quality of partnership

It is my perception that the application of a collaborative approach to learning provides real opportunities to develop naturally within this value system, and into which the formative principles of the National Literacy Strategy might be absorbed.

Rationalising collaborative learning in whole class and group teaching

Language development in collaborative learning contexts can embrace a variety of language teaching/learning activities and tasks. English teaching in Fleetville JM is both a subject to be studied in its own right and a medium to be explored and developed through which other learning is made possible.

The first premise – that English is a subject to be studied in its own right and that this can be achieved by combining whole-class teaching and collaborative learning in small groups – perfectly suits the daily literacy hour. This work took place in the autumn term 1998 with my Year 5 class of that year and shows how children can collaborate in their learning in any one lesson for as long as the teacher decides to allocate. In other words, collaborative learning can be applied to fifteen minutes, group work within a one-hour lesson or to a longer project.

The exploration of language as a learning medium in whole class teaching and collaborative learning groups can also be part of a longer project as it was with my Year 5 class of 1996. This class was used to a mixture of whole-class teaching and group-work activities in the school so pupils were familiar with the routine by the time they joined me in Year 5. But the group work we had been practising, I discovered, was quite different to collaborative learning of the kind we are espousing in this book.

I had been very concerned that in our normal group work some pupils made little contribution. Some pupils appeared to dominate not only the activities allocated to them but also the verbal feedback to the whole class. It seemed sensible not to force the apparently unwilling pupils to perform in front of their peers for fear of placing them in embarassing situations.

I was also concerned that no matter how long some children were given to complete a task, they never seemed to manage. This was true of pupils who spoke English as a first language and the bilingual children who were at varying degrees of proficiency in English. So I decided to adopt the collaborative learning approach, which would embrace what I had always done – whole class teaching and group work – but with a structure which would support the achievement of all the children in my class.

Two learning contexts are described below, in which whole-class teaching and collaborative learning were successfully combined in two Year 5 classrooms:

*   Within-project work during which language was studied as a learning medium: this means that understanding the language we use in any subject area is crucial. In this project we want full comprehension of what an exhibition is, in both its historical and its social context. Later on, geographical terms are explored to create an imaginary world of shipwreck and survival; the use of geographical terms with their appropriate meaning is a requirement of the Geography National Curriculum programme at KS2, page 10.

*   In two literacy hours during which a language structure – the future tense, prescribed in the National Literacy Strategy programme for Year 5, term 1, page 45 – was explored as a study of language in its own right.

First, however, I must clarify two aspects of this work:

The first is that a collaborative approach to learning supports language development in the classroom in the following ways:

*   by extending contexts for learning – thereby first enabling and then affirming the value of a range of skills for Investigating language appropriate to the task by

> analysing its applicability
> discussing with group peers its use in the given context
> reaching consensus on the linguistic items that have been selected
> recording the group's agreement
> demonstrate individual and group's understanding

*   by extending children's ability to work independently

- by providing a range of structured possibilities towards gathering and expressing individual ideas and opinions

- by facilitating the possibility of real interactive learning

- by clarifying and extending vocabulary

- by affirming the value of a variety of individual contributions within a group context and thereby building self-esteem

- by enabling purposeful social interaction and thereby

> honing social skills
> fine-tuning learning skills
> > developing good listening
> > sharing ideas and opinions
> > 'challenging' in a positive way

- by providing a range of clearly communicated and achievable success criteria;

> putting learning objectives in 'childspeak' by setting group targets and setting individual targets within the group.

The second is Defining principles of collaborative learning

To elicit the best responses and learning outcome from all the children in my class both the children and I had to be clear about the nature of this teaching/learning approach. It was important that the children were able to accept this approach. To do this we needed to speak the same language i.e. we needed to reach a consensus of understanding of the processes involved. The children had to participate in some of the decision-making processes, especially when these pertained to definitions of crucial terms: for example, 'what do you mean by discussing, or role, or recording?'

What follows is a check-list of procedures which I carried out with my Year 5 class of 1996.

- the aims and purposes of collaborative learning were made explicit to the children.

- Children were taught to work in groups.

- Small group work was very carefully defined and structured in terms of:

> activities – in the context of a developmental programme
> allocated roles – to facilitate peer support
> purposeful well-focused contributions – to enable a working understanding of the various roles that participants can play within a group
> timing

- I tried to structure every lesson in terms of:

communicated learning objectives

cycle of review – by asking the following questions:

> 'How are we getting on?'
>
> 'How well are we working together?'
>
> 'What can we do together to improve?'
>
> 'Let's share what we have achieved'

Whole-class teaching and collaborative learning

There are three parts to this section:

The two Year 5 classes are described and the two projects are placed in the school's curriculum plan and in the National Curriculum requirements. The collaborative learning programme is presented

The Classrooms

Number of pupils: 1996/97 – 26
1998/99 – 35

Layout of the classroom: the children were given work stations in the classroom, so that they could work around tables within a given area. These areas were arranged so that the children could easily face forward to enable full individual or group participation in whole class instruction or plenary sessions.

Languages spoken: Urdu, Panjabi, Tamil and English

Ability levels: the majority of pupils were consistently operating at National Curriculum Level 4. The bilingual children were generally assessed as achieving at Level 3, and to be demonstrating less confidence and therefore less effectiveness in the context of 'freely structured' class discussion or group work.

Approach to English teaching and learning: the collaborative learning project of 1996/7 was specifically constructed to support the extension of language skills by presenting a carefully structured range of learning activities. These were designed to enable a developing and valued level of contribution from all the children. These activities were planned into a cross-curricular context whereby the extension of language skills formed an intrinsic part of each lesson's learning objectives. This approach translated relatively easily into the language specific structure of the National Literacy Strategy – Year 5 1998/99 – with its parallel emphasis on definition of task and clarity.

The project in the school's curriculum plan

The collaborative learning focus – Year 5 1996/97 – was, after a discrete period of introduction, incorporated into the Year 5 section of the whole school topic plan, informing learning across one geography and one history topic. The geography topic investigated an overseas location, Saint Lucia and the history was the Victorians, both fulfilling the National Curriculum requirements. In 1998/99 teaching and learning principles which were made explicit through the 1996/97 programme continued to inform a cross-curricular approach, whilst also achieving a defined expression in response to the requirements of the National Literacy Strategy.

The collaborative learning programme

The first two lessons of the 1996/97 collaborative project were designed to teach the children to work together towards a common goal. This process would involve an approach that would be unfamiliar to the children and would require them to change their attitudes towards themselves and their peers.

This section of the programme provided an open period of exploration and experimentation in which specific structures were introduced, learning objectives made explicit. An open learning culture was encouraged, with particular emphasis on the key, creative contribution of each child. On-going aspects of the programme – its translation into more specific curriculum terms – found natural expression and extension within this developing culture of partnership and shared achievement.

The 1996-97collaborative learning programme

I devised a three-phase cycle to this programme. In phase 1 the children and I would investigate what is involved in collaborative learning. As neither the children nor I had worked like this before I thought that it would, in itself, be a process of collaborative learning if we could explore together what is involved and what is required of each member of the class in this approach to teaching and learning. New rules would need to be devised and a completely novel way of conceptualising group dynamics applied. Two lessons, each of a half a morning session, were devoted to this process.

In phase two we applied the collaborative learning approach to the project we were already immersed in: The Victorians. We had investigated the socio-economic and historical aspect of the topic and were in the middle of looking at the role of exhibitions in the context of a particular period. We wanted to find out:

- What is an exhibition?
- What does the term actually mean?
- What goes into an exhibition?
- How is that decided?
- What does an exhibition represent?

Such questions involved a huge amount of investigation into the historical semantics of the English language. The meanings of terms may change according to the times in which they are used. So we decided to look at the Great Exhibition of 1851 and how it might differ from an Exhibition 2000 – which would incorporate Our World in the 90s – which we would hold in our school. This would lead us into studying the language of advertising as we worked on advertising posters for this school exhibition. We were lucky that our head-teacher remembered visiting the Festival of Britain of 1951 as a young boy and was able to give a brief talk to my class about his impressions and memories of that experience.

In phase three we had the opportunity to use our geography project – the island of St Lucia – to imagine ourselves shipwrecked on a desert island on which everything had to start from scratch if we were to survive. The most important starting point was to establish a code of conduct by establishing collaborative working groups with straightforward, clear and simple rules to follow. Everyone had to play a vital role in the survival process until we were (hopefully!) rescued.

The three-phase programme looked like this:

Phase One – Preparing for collaborative work
(Lessons 1 and 2)

- Allocate collaborative home groups

- Explain the aims of sharing and learning

- Set task 1 to the groups: how best can we learn? Make up a group's list

- Set task 2 to the groups: devise your own group rules to which you must conform because you are devising them yourself

Phase Two – The Victorians
(Lessons 3 and 4)

- Context: investigating the Great Exhibition of 1851

- Our World in the 1990s: home research sheets – pupils to take these sheets home and complete them with the help of family members

- Exhibition 2000 – our school's exhibition for which each group will design a brochure

- Media/Advertising – each group to make a poster for Exhibition 2000

Phase Three – Overseas Location – The island of St Lucia
(adapted from Stephens, 1985)
(Lessons 5, 6, and 7)

- tropical island – research key facts

- tropical island – draw a map

- on the island – a range of group activities take place:

  > setting up camp
  > salvage
  > who does what?
  > building a shelter
  > inventing games
  > rules and punishment
  > rescue!

PHASE ONE – PREPARING FOR COLLABORATIVE LEARNING
Lesson 1 – Sharing and Learning – 1hr
Language focus – semantics of collaboration, consensus, discussion

Learning objectives
- to explain why the class will be working in small groups

- to share ideas on how best we learn

- to provide each group with the opportunity to arrive at a 'consensus' list

- to consider each group's ideas as a whole class – and thereby reinforce the shared meaning of the session

- to encourage involvement from all the children.

Procedures involved
- Allocate working groups. The class of 26 children was divided into six working groups: two groups of five children each and four groups of four children each. This was done in advance so when the lesson started the groups were already shown on the board. I allocated children to the groups so they were mixed ability and had the skills required for the collaborative tasks. The roles needed for this lesson were: one scribe, a chairperson to manage group discussion, and a reporter – the person responsible for communicating the results of the group discussion to the rest of the class.

The children were not consulted as to which group they would like to work in. The selection was successful in the sense that the group dynamics appeared to be positive across the six groups. The groups were identified as groups A, B, C, D, E, F. Not very original but they do not denote any kind of ability level at all in their neutral labelling!

- Give a timed structure to the lesson. This is important in collaborative learning. Children work more efficiently if they are given a tight framework within which to execute a task. And the teacher gets less time to prevaricate and pays more attention to focusing everybody's attention on the required tasks. Consequently children get more talk time in the lesson. This first lesson was thus timed:

15 minutes whole-class teacher-led discussion on why we are
- learning together in small groups.
- Consider how best we learn: make a preliminary class-list as an example of what they will do in group work.

10 minutes individual work – in their draft-work books write down four ways that each considers to be best for learning and give reasons for the choices made.

5 minutes collaborative group work – each group meets and each member of the group reads out his/her list and the reasons.

5 minutes collaborative group work –
- discuss the merits of the lists

- combine the individual lists into one group list

- the scribe writes down the group's definitive list

10 minutes collaborative group work –
- each group to prioritise its list of how best we learn in order of importance by giving asterisks to the degree of importance of each learning strategy on the list on a scale from four down to zero.

- each group could choose its own method of prioritising its how-best-to-learn list.

15 minutes whole class teacher-led discussion – look together at each of the six lists and discuss common aspects; make the lists available to be typed so that copies can be distributed to all the groups

- Assessment of the lesson – the children settled very well to the task, appearing to understand why we were working in small groups and functioning and sharing positively within their groups.

- Results – six group lists on This is how we learn

HOW BEST DO WE LEARN?
CONSIDERATION OF CHILDREN'S FINDINGS

The breadth of the children's findings indicates the scope and quality of their discussions, whereby an initially abstract idea was rapidly interpreted in terms of the children's own experience to become a firmly owned, concrete series of group lists.

In the plenary session that concluded the range of initial discussions, considerable interest was generated by the generally lowly place afforded to the explicit role of teaching in the learning process. The groups tended to apportion a greater significance to an individualised model of learning. This was often evident in the way children focused on the potential of technology as a learning resource. This finding provided an interesting insight into the children's 'learning self-image', the groups presenting a developed picture of themselves as independent learners.

However, corporate aspects of learning through such other people as parents, siblings, extended family, friends and so on are also evident, providing integrity and logic to the project.

PHASE ONE – PREPARING FOR COLLABORATIVE LEARNING
Lesson 2 – The rules for group collaborative work – one hour

Language focus – semantics of rules, commonality/similarity,
rules for different settings

Learning objectives

*   to build on the progress made in Lesson on 1
*   to provide the children with an opportunity for reflection on their experience and assessment of their achievement
*   to produce a model towards extending that achievement in terms of Rules for group work

Lesson structure

15 minutes whole class reflection – teacher-led discussion:

*   What went well yesterday? How could we improve the way we worked or how could we repeat our success?
*   think about rules: what are rules?
*   can we think of any examples?
*   why do we need rules?
*   do we need rules for collaborative group work?
*   what would these rules be?

HOW BEST DO WE LEARN?
The findings of six groups

GROUP A

Books	***
The teacher	***
Remembering	***
Listening	***
Study topics	**
Mum and dad	**
Practice	**
Doing things	**
Television	**
Grandparents	**
Other people	**
Radio	*
Writing	*
Uncle	*

GROUP B

Computers	***
Memory	***
Dictionaries	***
Thinking	***
Teacher's help	***
Research	***
Thesaurus	***
Videos	**
Studying	**
Television	**
Study topics	**
Parents' help	**
Grandparents	**
Overhearing	**
From music	**
Watching people	*
Tape recorder	*

GROUP C

By doing things	***
Study topics	***
Reading books	***
From grandparents	***
Talking to parents	**
Listening	**
Computer software	**
Remembering	**
Practice	**
Research	**
Repetition	**
Videos	*
Listening to tapes	*

GROUP D

Books	***
Other people	***
Learning times table	***
Computers	***
Listening to the teacher	***
Remembering	***
Asking questions	***
Mum and dad	***
Grandparents	***
Calculators	***
Writing things down	***
Doing things	**
Study topics	**
Encyclopaedia	**
Television	**
Dictionary	**
Brothers	

GROUP E

Books	***
Listening	***
Doing work	***
Family	***
Cassettes and records	***
Computer	***
Thinking	***
Television	***
Teacher	**
Study topics	**
Videos	**
Remembering	**
Asking questions	**
Writing things down	**
Reading again and again	**
Doing things	**
Answering questions	*

GROUP F

Television	***
Books	***
Parents	***
Videos	***
Understanding what teacher says	**
Computers	**
Study topics	**
Grandparents	**
Practice	**
Remembering	*
Doing	*

10 minutes Individual work – with notebooks
• make a list of five rules that you would like your group to consider

20 minutes Collaborative group work – reach consensus on rules for your group
• each person to present own list of rules

• make a new group list by writing down the common or similar rules:

• this involves discussing the meaning of words used in the individual list

• think about the remaining rules, i.e. those left in any of the individual list: does the group want to include any of them? Why?

15 minutes Whole class discussion – each group to report as follows:
• the designated group reporters to read out their group's lists

• the teacher to write down on a large sheet on easel/board all the common points resulting from individual groups' lists to create class rules to be implemented during collaborative learning

• all children to receive a copy of their respective group's rules list for their own files

• the class rules will be placed centrally in the classroom for reference

Assessment of the lesson

All the children, including the bilingual pupils, participated in the groups' discussions. There was a great deal of observation made on the importance of listening, reaching consensus, speaking firmly but quietly and especially no arguments!

It is worth quoting the comment made about the individual participation of two of the bilingual children, made by my Section 11 colleague who observed these children very closely.

'A (Group D) [...] certainly contributed to [the] discussion, taking his turn to speak rather than leading on any point. [He] was more able to add to the discussion when one member [of the group] went round the group in turn to include everyone'. Clearly, then, the underlying principle of collaborative learning is quickly put into practice by the children and it obviously works: – that each member of the group should have a role to play to ensure cohesion and true equality of opportunity in the interactive learning process.

'M (Group E) [...] appeared to see himself as part of the group as he seemed attentive at all times and tried to read [the] notes as they were scribed'.

Outcome The table of rules opposite indicate the amount of thought and commitment which every child contributed to the discussion.

RULES FOR COLLABORATIVE LEARING DEVISED BY EACH GROUP

GROUP A
Sharing and Learning

1. always listen to other people
2. always include other people
3. don't argue too much but sort things out with discussion
4. don't make comments
5. always talk quietly
6. share your thoughts
7. never shout
8. take turns
10. don't speak too much
11. if people think it's wrong, then vote

GROUP B
Sharing and Learning

1. don't all talk at once
2. make sure everyone is included
3. agree on everything we write down
4. ask for everybody's opinion
5. always listen to each other
6. don't be rude about what other people say
7. say your comment and then be quiet
8. don't disturb other groups
9. don't call people names

GROUP C
Sharing and Learning

1. always listen to each other
2. make sure everyone is included
3. take turns to speak
4. do not argue
5. don't agree with someone else's comment if you've got a different comment
6. just talk about what you're doing

GROUP D
Sharing and Learning

1. always listen to one another
2. make sure everyone is included
3. make sure that everyone has their turn
4. be honest about what you think
5. if we disagree then vote
6. take great interest
7. don't argue
8. don't just think about what you think is right

GROUP E
Sharing and Learning

1. always listen to one another
2. make sure that everyone is included
3. don't argue
4. do not be horrible to one another
5. share ideas
6. take turns
7. don't make horrible comments
8. don't shout at each other
9. work together

GROUP F
Sharing and Learning

1. don't shout out
2. always listen to each other
3. make sure that everyone is included
4. when you want to speak put your hand up
5. don't be silly
6. don't tease people in your group
7. discuss your decisions
8. only listen to people with their hand up
9. don't argue
10. don't say silly things

PHASE TWO – THE VICTORIANS – HISTORY
NATIONAL CURRICULUM
Lesson 3 – Exhibitions – 2 hours 10 minutes (whole morning)

Language focus- the term exhibition in its historical and
socio-economic context

Learning objectives

- to make the meaning of the word 'EXHIBITION' real through exploration, discussion and a sharing of experience
- to provide a step-by-step approach towards further supporting the range of co-operation developing within each home-group
- to facilitate the creative involvement of each child in the class via:
     carefully designed tasks
     clearly stated roles
- to provide the opportunity for whole class reflection and involvement at key moments during the morning's activities

CHILDSPEAK – here are our aims for this morning

- to share our understanding of the word EXHIBITION: do you know what it means? Can you think of some examples?
- to work successfully in our home groups: has your group made good progress on its tasks?
- to share: has everyone in your group really shared in a way that they are happy with? Has everyone kept thinking about your Group Rules?
- to see how the different parts of our work fit together. Are you clear about what you are going to do next?

Learning Context

- Topic: The Victorians
- Theme: The Great Exhibition 1851

Lesson structure

Session one
10 minutes whole-class teacher-led discussion on the word EXHIBITION:
- search for a meaning;
- remind spokes-person and scribe of each collaborative group of their roles as well as that of the working partners;
- decide the order of reporting by the groups later in the morning;

10 minutes groups at work stations –

- the scribe of the group to remind the group of the rules it devised for successful collaboration

- discuss the exhibitions we have visited i.e. MOMI and the Museum of St. Albans on Hatfield Road; scribe to write down the group's observations

25 minutes whole-class teacher-led discussion during which each group's spokesperson

- will report back on the group's discussions

- direct pupils' attention to the flip-chart, next to the teacher, on which the words THE GREAT EXHIBITION are written and ponder aloud on what was so special about it? Why was it called The Great Exhibition?

- report back on MOMI (The Museum of the Moving Image in London) – what was special about that exhibition?

  What do the children remember most clearly about MOMI?

  Each group's spokesperson to give the group's impressions and findings.

- report back on how one can find out about exhibitions: what might be the best way? What did we learn about how to do this from the St Alban's Museum? Each spokesperson to present the group's suggested methods

- teacher to present work to be done by groups in the next group learning on OUR WORLD IN THE 90s, i.e. discuss and come up with suggestions on how to put together an exhibition of our own world in the 1990s.

15 minutes home groups at work stations –

- share the evidence i.e. with the information gathered at home on the sheets of OUR WORLD IN THE 90s

- put together a group's content list for what could be exhibited in a 90s exhibition which could best represent our life as we are living it from many aspects: technology, information, leisure, education, family, environment, fashion and transport

- the scribe to compile a group's list and the group's suggestions on how to get more information about putting together this exhibition: use the KEY FACTS SHEET for this.

Session two

10 minutes whole-class review of what has been learned so far about EXHIBITIONS

- does everybody understand what this is? What its purpose is? What it means?

- set new group task: design a brochure for the exhibition of our world in the 90s

- allocate new roles to the members of the working groups: each group will have one scribe, one spokesperson and two/three working partners. Depending on whether there are four or five people in the group, there will be two or three working partners and this will affect the allocation of roles. All members of the group will initially be allocated a working partner, these later developing into dual roles at the time of the group's internal – within group – feedback, in which case one member of one partnership will record and collate the whole group's response to the completed task while the other member of the partnership prepares to report these findings to the whole class in the plenary session. Working partners will be allocated dual roles as part of a rolling programme designed to enable equal accessibility to each role for all the children

30 minutes collaborative work on the brochure – four activities, each to be undertaken by one group member: design the brochure, draw cartoons for different sections of the exhibition, write captions for each cartoon, cut and paste. In the groups of five, two pupils will work together on the design or the writing

10 minutes whole-class assessment – sharing of key facts collated by the groups' scribes at the end of session one above

20 minutes whole-class – listen to the headteacher talking about visiting the 1951 Festival of Britain as a young child; an opportunity for children to realise that writing history is a real-life process and not confined to printed history books.

Lesson 4 – Making a poster for the exhibition 2000 –
2 hours 10 minutes (whole morning)
Language focus – Exploring the language of advertising

Learning objectives
- to feed the results of partnership work into the larger group to facilitate and reinforce a sense of group identity and purpose
- to explore and understand new vocabulary: especially the following three terms audience, format, persuade, to understand their linguistic meaning and their implication in the design of the poster and advertising in general
- to understand how the identity of a target audience prefigures a particular approach
- to negotiate collaboratively the groups' roles in making the poster
- to achieve a sense of progression from inanimate poster to television advertising

OUR WORLD IN THE 90s

Television	Computers and
Film: Video	Communications

Holidays and Travel	1990-1996
	Learning and School
	My learning journey

My family	Houses and Homes

Cars and Transport	Fashion

This task sheet was set for homework the previous week. The information gathered by each child is to be shared and discussed by home groups in the Phase two lesson. From this discussion each group is to draw a group's list of key facts – and write it in the Key Facts Sheet for Our World in the 90s exhibition. This had only two boxes: 'Our focus' and 'Where we might find some information'.

CHILDSPEAK

- to share our partner work with the rest of the groups

- to learn and understand the meaning of these words: AUDIENCE, FORMAT, PERSUADE

- to think how we can make our work real to all the people we want to understand it

- to make sure everyone in our group gets a fair chance to share and that everyone listens carefully to everyone else

- to be happy with the progress we've made on our EXHIBITION 2000 poster

- to know how what we've done today will join onto what we're going to do next

Lesson structure

Session one

10 minutes whole-class – explain to the class today's objectives with particular reference to a new role in the groups – an editor, who will help to record the decisions made by the group in terms of tasks identified and allocated; the editor will also collate the work produced, keep a record of progress made and chair discussions at specific stages of development

20 minutes home-groups at work stations –
- each pair to identify the meaning of the words audience and format

- in each group pupils will work in pairs to consider the targeted audience for the poster and the most persuasive format

10 minutes whole-class – teacher-led discussion on advertising campaign to inform and entice the selected audience, with each group's spokesperson taking it in turn to present briefly the group's initial ideas
- attention is drawn by the teacher to four aspects to be considered by the groups when working on the poster: lettering, illustrations, writing/ information giving, and exhibition logo

20 minutes home-groups at work stations –
- each group to decide on the roles to be undertaken by each of its members and the editor writes them down – the roles are:

  - graphic artist for lettering
  - illustrator
  - content writer
  - artist for drawing the logo
  - the poster must include the following information: venue, date, price
  - other information is to be decided by the groups

Session two

25 minutes home-groups at work stations – making the posters

10 minutes whole-class teacher-led discussion: turning a poster into a television advertisement

* what would we have to consider? Would our audience be the same? What about the format?

15 minutes whole-class watch advertisement in television room with stimulus task sheet;

* questions to think about: who is the advertisement for?

* How do they persuade us to buy?

Assessment of lesson

The children worked constructively and according to our learning aims. The change of roles within the groups in this session made for a positive transition from the information to the practical stages of the lesson. The children were stretched by today's activities by being exposed to more sophisticated language. No child seemed to be reticent in class discussions, indicating, possibly, that they find the content of the lesson and this way of working stimulating. A great deal of new language was learnt today by all the children: the language of advertising.

PHASE THREE – OVERSEAS LOCATION – THE ISLAND OF ST LUCIA GEOGRAPHY NATIONAL CURRICULUM

In phase three, our collaborative learning programme was transferred to yet another curriculum area, geography. There are three lessons in this phase, lessons 5, 6 and 7. By now the format of the lessons must have become very familiar. Each lesson always started with whole-class sessions, which allowed for recap of both the content of the programme and the way we were learning together. I felt it was important to keep drawing the children's attention to the collaborative nature of their group activities. Just as any other learning behaviour – listening to the teacher, voice level, being neat and tidy, and so on – needs to be constantly reinforced. It is vital that children are reminded of the nature of team-work in collaborative learning. Good habits become ingrained with continued approval and reminding, just as bad habits can become the norm if they are not admonished.

Lesson 7 is presented in full in the following pages. A resume of lessons 5 and 6 will be sufficient to indicate the continuity of the programme which has been focusing on subject specific language, shared learning processes and shared outcomes. Of particular interest will be the assessment of children's responses to collaboration. Note the change in teacher control of the learning situation and see what happens when children are given responsibility for decision making in the group learning in lesson 5.

Lesson 5 – The island –
2 hours 10 minutes (whole morning)
Language focus – subject-specific geographical terms

Learning objectives
*   for each group to draw information/knowledge from one another in order to present their own key facts relevant to their own model of a tropical island

*   for each group to engage in discussion and show evidence of negotiating some outcome

*   to understand the components of a map and to begin to incorporate these – and the previously gathered information – onto a tropical island map

Lesson structure
whole-class teacher-directed discussion:
*   introduce the key-facts sheet defining vocabulary: what does climate mean? What are exports/imports? Can we identify those different but joining parts which together make 'economy?' This should provide 'spark points' to stimulate discussion

*   give clues about how a series of answers might connect to provide an over-view, an information bank from which to construct the map eg. on the fact sheet the children select the name of a capital city, which will then be located on their outline plan, having parallel reference to other details such as the nature of the surrounding terrain, the accessibility of water and the quality of communications

collaborative group work:
*   to begin discussion on the key-facts sheet

whole class review:
*   of key-facts sheet

collaborative group work:
*   complete key facts sheets

*   draw the tropical island map

Assessment of the lesson
This proved to be an interesting session on a number of counts:

*   The pre-set structure of the group was more open than for any task set so far. The scribes were not given any specific remit and this led to some interesting results. Some scribes were very proactive while others behaved as passive recorders of the group's agreed opinions and suggestions. This

---

TROPICAL ISLAND – KEY FACTS

- Our island's name –

- Climate in summer –

- Climate in winter –

- The capital city is –

- The population is –

- The main language is –

- Most people earn their living by –

- The main exports are –

- The main imports are –

- Landmarks on the island –

---

factor affected the direction and tone of many group discussions during the Key Facts sessions.

- In one group cracks began to appear on the collaborative surface. One child, feeling that she was not being heard and that the scribe was not being responsive to the whole group, was reduced to tears. Other groups experienced difficulty at the decision-making stage although they had been quite democratic about information gathering. For example: what do you do if you decide to determine choice through a vote and the vote is a draw? (Ultimate answer was: determine a new choice altogether: return to the original range of options and select another example from those provided by the group at the initial discussion stage).

- To enable the children to begin to cover the cracks themselves, my Section 11 colleague and I worked closely with some groups in order to:

  - define the actual difficulties

- discuss ways of solving them

- be a presence whilst the children begin implementing these strategies.

By applying different aspects of this approach many groups successfully completed the initial tasks. Thus the collaborative process carried the learning.

- The children moved readily into the paired work stage of the morning and the atmosphere in the classroom became very positive.

- The whole-class feedback session contributed significantly to refocusing and positively directing the morning.

- There was a sense that the children's learning was enhanced as a result of being able to measure any initial problems identified on the way, against a range of suggested 'solving strategies' – i.e. 'if we continue to disagree as to a best option, we accept that a majority vote will determine our group's final choice'. The fact that these strategies were supported by a clearly stated external structure – 'you have thirty minutes to complete this given task, after which time each group will report back to the whole class' – invigorated decision making and this live and honest collaborative process produced excellent outcomes.

Lesson 6 – Setting up camp on the island – one hour
Language focus – making choices and explaining them

Learning objectives
- to develop clear class discussion and shared decision making

- to build upon the tropical island map exercise

- to provide a clear aim and to facilitate the structuring of group discussions

- for each group to complete the tasks in the set time

Lesson structure
whole-class – present today's work to the class and ascertain that every pupil knows what to do: i.e. select four possible sites to set up camp on the island

pair-work – children to work in partner groups, determining options for the location of their camp with reference to the Tropical Island map produced in the last session

whole-class plenary – how have we done so far? Each group to report back using the 'Setting up camp' prompt sheet as a shared point of reference

---

Setting up camp

Place:

Our reasons for this choice:

Other possible sites:

-

-

-

Why did we choose these sites?

-

-

-

How did the bilingual children perform in this lesson?

All three children (S, M, and L) appeared to be taking good note of the teacher-led whole-class discussion at the beginning of the lesson. S most of all had 'his hand up in response to most questions' and L 'sometimes', whereas M 'did not volunteer' although he knew exactly what was expected of him in the group work activity and completed what was required of him.

The group activity required a great deal of 'selection, reasoning, justifying', during which S was 'able to contribute to finding a solution once his understanding was clear eg. 'this is a good place, it's near water' (pointing to the sea). His partner indicated that they needed fresh water once it was realised that sea water was salt water.

L appeared to have benefited the most from this lesson's collaborative process. He developed a 'very good partnership with his partner. [He was] able to reason quite fluently and their discussion process was very active. L finds working with a partner more productive than contributing to a larger group'.

Lesson 7 – Establishing life on the island – 2 hours 10 minutes
(whole morning)
Language focus – understand concepts hidden in terms
such as staged planning

Learning objectives – CHILDSPEAK

- to complete the 'our camp' jigsaw and make this week's piece EXACTLY fit last week's piece

- to give our best attention to our work partner and to the person who is talking in our group

- we want everyone to feel that they are being listened to

- to listen carefully to all instructions and try to win the challenge of completing every task inside its special time

- to feel pleased about our group's contribution to 'Who does what?'

Lesson structure

Session one

10 minutes whole-class – teacher-led discussion on today's learning objectives: these are on an easel and written large for everyone to read; the class will look at these objectives during the day to see if they are being fulfilled:

- have an overview of the whole project

- understand learning objectives

- explain the 'camp' task and allocate scribes

- the groups must decide on materials (to build a shelter), and how to build it and who's going to be doing what on the island (who does what?)

- remind the class to imagine that the whole project is a jigsaw puzzle and today's piece will have to fit in with the pieces of the previous lessons on this project

- remember how important listening is so that instructions are clearly understood (in whole-class discussions) and other people's words are valued (in group work)

10 minutes pair-work – plan the building of a shelter

- with task sheet 'Building a shelter 1' decide on what the shelter will look like and draw it

- discuss with your partner the materials you will need for the shelter you want

- one of you – who is for you to decide – will be the scribe of the partnership

5 minutes whole-class plenary – how are we getting on?

- Remind pupils that they need to have in mind task sheet 'Building a shelter 2' while still working on sheet 1. Sheet 2 asks them to design the building of the shelter – as they have designed it – in four stages so they must have the stages of construction in mind when designing the shelter and thinking of materials: the three processes are interlocked

25 minutes pair-work to continue

10 minutes whole-class plenary – how did we get on?

- what learning objectives on today's list of objectives have we achieved so far?

- invite some pupils to present the design of their pair's shelter and list of materials needed and explain how they reached the decision

Session two
15 minutes pair-work – complete planning the building of the shelter, moving on to the four stages of the construction process

5 minutes whole-class plenary –

- stop planning the shelter work and move on to thinking about establishing and sustaining life on this desert island – what jobs will be needed to sustain life – task sheet 1 'Who does what?'

- decide in your home groups how these jobs are going to be done and by whom? task sheet 2 of 'Who does what?'

10 minutes individual work –

- island: make a list of jobs that need doing on the island on task sheet 1

5 minutes whole-class plenary – ask some children to read out their own lists

15 minutes home groups at work stations

- From the lists made by individuals, decide on top ten jobs that need doing

- decide who's going to do the jobs on task sheet 2

10 minutes whole-class – each group presents own work to the rest of the class.

Comments on the task sheet
Building a shelter (2)

Every lesson produces surprises in the seemingly most harmless areas of learning. Who would have thought that the word stage, or, to be more precise, the phrase doing it in stages would present obstacles to understanding? This lesson was video-recorded and the transcript of part of it shows what happened. We are at part a) of the whole-class plenary at the end of session one (See lesson plan).

[T = teacher; P = any pupil talking; other capital letters refer to an individual child; xxx refer to inaudible speech]

Transcript

T: now then, here's a question some children have asked, *if we're moving to the next planned stage, what does that mean?* Why have we got stage one, stage two, stage three and stage four on our sheets?

Pupils' hands are up

Would anybody like to explain what they think that means? So that we can make sure we all understand when we start after break? Yes R.

R: Uhm, oh, I forgot it now

T: It's not that easy to, to explain, I mean, I know what I was thinking of when I wrote down stage one, stage two, but it does need explaining, I found that out this morning when I went walking around talking with you. M?

M: xxx uh, does it mean, uh, sort of splitting up so that each part xxx

T: Thank you, that's really a helpful start xxx splitting up; anybody else?

Pupils' hands are up

T: Yes D

D: Does it, uhm, stage one, xxx pick up the materials xxx so the first thing you do when you build it…

T: The first thing you do when you build it, so what's stage two then?

D: The second

Class laughs

T: OK, and so we can go on can't we?

My observations

I discovered this lack of understanding earlier in the session during the pair work activities as I eavesdropped on the children's discussions about their plans for the shelter.

Yes, I had not anticipated this word to be problematic. How does one explain a word which we believe is self-explanatory simply because we know what it means?

I want the children to think beyond division of a whole into parts, which is what M is saying here; they need to understand the concept of development which is sequential and in which one thing must be done before something else can be started.

D is right of course and so is the laughter of the rest of the class, which indicates that some of the children understood the contextual nature of my question. D is linguistically and mathematically correct in saying that stage two is the second stage in the sequence. How many children, like D, did not understand the broader and in-context question with which I meant 'What happens in stage two'? in the sequence of the planned design?

Pupils' hands are up

T: Yes L

L: xxx other people can help you make it

T: That's a very good point as well

Xxx

P: xxx get the bread?

T: really?

P: xxx get the bread?

T: Butter? Really?

Children laugh

T: You are making a shelter!

P: xxx

T: That's like saying stage one, perhaps that's like saying stage one is – tying sticks together [?] – xxx

But really? The first thing I have to do...

P: Get the materials

T: Right, so, what's that then? If I'm making a cheese sandwich

P: Get bread

P: And butter

T: Get the materials; stage two, let's get back to you N, what's stage two? Now I've got my bread and my cheese, what's next then?

P: [laughs] Butter it!

T: Right, that's making more sense to me now!

P: Cut the bread

T: So stage two is cut the bread, so what's stage three N then?

P: Put the cheese on

T: Right, now we come to the really interesting part

One pupil introduces the analogy of making a sandwich and the stages involved

I decide to work on the children's analogy – it's a good one, familiar to the children. So I am drawing on the children's experiences of making a sandwich to ensure understanding of the staging process since we cannot take for granted that children are able to transfer, without being taught to do so, a linguistic and/or cognitive skill from one area of life and/or curriculum to another.

Children laugh

T: What's stage four going to be?

P: xxx

T: If what we are doing is going to be successfull, it's going to have an end result, what's it going to be?

P: Eat it

P: Eat them

T: Eat the sandwich, and in your case, stage one, stage two, stage three and stage four [put your hands down] are going to end up in a shelter that's complete, aren't they? A shelter that's, not only complete, but actually we can say *this is something that people can really live in*, tell me, what difficulty are you going to have on a tropical island?

P: Uhm, the rain getting in the shelter

T: We've done lots of work on the weather, haven't we? Thank you A, it's worth thinking about...OK, I'll explain stage one, stage two, stage three, stage four, we've gone through it together.. after break, what you do is, you take your design and think how you are going to make this work and I'll give you fifteen minutes and then you'll be going onto individual tasks and change what they are thinking about

I quickly make the connection between the different stages involved in making a sandwich and the preparative stages of making a shelter. I make a link between the children's own experiences of the world and an imaginary problem. This problem had appeared to the children to be full of obstacles only because it presented difficulties at the linguistic level. The implications for ensuring that children understand the language of instructions and the language embedded in cognitive processes are obvious.

Task sheet Who does What? (2) deals with 'How we think we should make decisions on the island'. The points to consider are:

• one leader?

• a small council?

• is everybody involved in every condition.

The second part of the sheet is headed: 'This is why we think our ideas would work.

THE COLLABORATIVE LEARNING PROJECT
CONCLUDING COMMENTS

Rationale for this approach

So why choose to develop a learning programme within which collaborative learning is given active, formative status? Why opt to make a 'learning omelette' – collect and measure the ingredients, take the risk of mixing them together, hoping that the unified result is a positive summation of its individual parts! – when a pristine, perfectly structured, 'no trouble', inescapably singular, boiled egg might present an equally appropriate means towards satisfying the targeted 'learning hunger'?

Perhaps at the centre of any rationale is collaborative learning's potential as an encouraging and inspiring agent towards professional creativity and as a means towards meeting a live and extended range of learning aims with outcomes which might be measurable. Measurable not just in terms of children's learning achieved, but of learning absorbed – in terms of process, as well as result, and representing a known celebration of a shared achievement.

My own experience indicates that there are certain key, identifiable aspects which, in combination, assist collaborative learning to function effectively. Perhaps they might be thought of here as a kind of oil, enabling, lubricating the process of learning.

Key practical/organisational aspects

* Clarity of purpose and focus should be clearly communicated to the children. The objectives must be regularly measured in terms of progress achieved during times of whole class assessment.

* Learning stations for each group allocated within the classroom.

* A process of rotating roles within each group, such as scribe, group communicator in the context of plenary sessions, observer, with responsibility for sharing perceptions of the group's current effectiveness, and so on.

* Clearly defined time limits for each aspect of the task setting out what each group will have achieved by the end of an allocated period and information about how that achievement will be assessed.

* The provision of open-ended structures to record work, such as might guide, but not inhibit, creativity.

A critical examination of my own practice shows that classrooms work best when children are motivated and understand the reason for their learning, which is realistic and within their own experience.

THE NATIONAL LITERACY HOUR

We have seen that a key element to the collaborative learning approach is the teacher's strict adherence to the timing of every activity. Timing is essential to keeping '...a sense of urgency and pace in the work and helps to maintain a direct and lively atmosphere in the class' (DfEE, 1998, p 10). It may also have been noted that other aspects to collaborative learning go hand-in-hand with the strategies recommended in Literacy Hour rationale. Referring again to page 8 of the National Literacy Strategy folder, these strategies include:

• direction
• demonstration
• modelling
• scaffolding
• explanation
• questioning
• initiating and guiding exploration
• investigating ideas
• discussing and arguing
• listening to and responding

How these strategies are fine-tuned in the teaching of the future tense to my Year 5 class of 1998/99 is now described. The future tense and auxiliary verbs are a Year 5/Term 1 requirement in the National Literacy Strategy. By fine-tuning I mean the how of all of the above strategies.

• how does one direct pupils' investigation of the future tense in our English language?

• how does one demonstrate and model the use of the future tense?

• how should we go about scaffolding the new learning? What aspect of the future tense should be taught when?

• how do you explain the grammatical function of the auxiliary verbs required in the future tense in English

The two lessons that follow conform to all the requirements of the National Literacy Hour:

• they combine whole-class and group/or individual/or pair-work activities

• they are strictly timed

• they approach the study of the future tense at the word, sentence and text level

In addition, these lesson plans illustrate the need for teaching certain grammatical aspects before others so that the relevant concepts can be understood.

For example, five aspects of the future tense are found in the text selected for the class to study, so only these five aspects are the focus of these lessons. They are presented in a logical order: positive aspect before negative aspect, the long form before the short form. Another aspect of the future tense, (for example the future perfect), is not included because it does not appear in the story. It would have to be taught in a subsequent lesson, now that the children are familiar with the basic future tense.

The timing of these two lessons on the future do not adhere strictly to the division of the Literacy Hour into quarters, though the times allocated to whole class and group/pair/individual activities approximate it. These lesson plans on the future keep the 'essential elements' of the Literacy Hour but have been adapted 'to meet the pupils' needs' (DfEE, 1998, p 10).

THE NATIONAL LITERACY HOUR
THE FUTURE and AUXILIARY VERBS

MATERIALS

COPY OF THE ORIGINAL STORY – The Librarian and the robbers, by Margaret Mahy 1978

ADAPTED STORY – The Librarian and the robbers – for use in the literacy hour – (reproduced on pages 123-125)

TEACHER'S REFERENCE SHEET – on future tense and auxiliary verbs

SENTENCE TASK SHEET FROM PRESENT TO FUTURE – to be used in the second pair work session

GROUP WORK TASK SHEET – to be used with the group work texts in the 20 minute group work session and in whole class feedback session at the end

GROUP WORK AUTHENTIC TEXTS

Two LITERACY HOUR lesson plans

SUGGESTIONS FOR USING THE MATERIALS

- Because the full text of the story in which the future is introduced is too long, I would read the story to the class during the week, just as a story, so they become familiar with it. It is better to introduce grammar in contexts already familiar to the pupils.

- The Librarian and the robbers has been adapted for use in the first part of the lesson, the first whole-class session. The story will be read together and the highlighted future verbal phrases will be used as an introductory class discussion.

- The TEACHER'S REFERENCE SHEET is there as a grammatical reference to the different aspects of the future which have been taken from the story; an OHT (overhead transparency) of this sheet can be used as a class reference during the class discussion on the future aspects.

- The GROUP WORK AUTHENTIC TEXTS for the long group-work session have been selected with differentiation in mind; different texts may be used with different groups; the texts are cross-curricular in order to train and emphasise transference of grammatical skills.

THE LIBRARIAN AND THE ROBBERS
Margaret Mahy, 1978

One day Serena Laburnum, the beautiful librarian, was carried off by wicked robbers. She had just gone for a walk in the woods at the edge of town, when the robbers came charging at her and carried her off.

'Why are you kidnapping me?' she asked coldly. 'I have no wealthy friends or relatives. Indeed I am an orphan with no real home but the library.'

'That's just it,' said the Robber Chief. 'The City Council **will pay** richly to have you restored. After all, everyone knows that the library does not work properly without you.'

This was especially true because Miss Laburnum had the library keys.

'I think I ought to warn you,' she said, 'that I spent the weekend with a friend of mine who has four little boys. Everyone in the house had the dread disease of Raging Measles.'

'That's all right!' said the Robber Chief, sneering a bit. 'I've had them.'

'But I haven't!' said the robber at his elbow, and the other robbers looked at Miss Laburnum uneasily. None of them had had the dread disease of Raging Measles.

As soon as the robbers' ransom note was received by the City Council, there was a lot of discussion. Everyone was anxious that things should be done in the right way.

'What is it when our librarian is kidnapped?' asked a councillor. 'Is it staff expenditure or does it come out of cultural funds?'

'The cultural committee **will meet** in a fortnight,' said the Mayor. 'I propose we let them make a decision on this.'

But long before that, all the robbers (except the Robber Chief) had Raging Measles.

First of all they became very irritable and had red sniffy noses.

'I *think* a hot bath brings out the rash,' said Miss Laburnum doubtfully. 'Oh, if only I were in my library I would be able to look up measles in my *Dictionary of Efficient and Efficacious Home Nursing*.'

The Robber Chief looked gloomily at his gang.

'Are you sure it's measles?' he said. 'That's a very undignified complaint for a robber to suffer from. There are few people who are improved by spots, but for robbers they are disastrous. Would you take a spotty robber seriously?'

'It is no part of a librarian's duty to take any robber seriously, spotty or otherwise,' said Miss Laburnum haughtily. 'And, anyhow, there WON'T BE any robbing until they have got over the Raging Measles. They are in quarantine. After all you don't want to be blamed for spreading measles everywhere, do you?'

The robber chief groaned.

'If you **will allow** me,' said Miss Laburnum, 'I **will go** to my library and borrow *The Dictionary of Efficient and Efficacious Home Nursing*. With the help of that invaluable book I **shall try** to alleviate the suffering of your fellows. Of course I **shall** only **be able** to take it out for a week. It is a special reference book, you see.'

The groaning of his fellows suffering from Raging Measles was more than the Robber chief could stand.

'All right,' he said. 'You can go and get that book, and **we'll call off** the kidnapping for the present. Just a temporary measure.'

In a short time Miss Laburnum was back with several books.

'A hot bath **will bring out** the rash!' she announced reading clearly and carefully. 'Then you must have the cave darkened, and you mustn't read or play cards. You have to be careful of your eyes when you have measles.'

The robbers found it very dull, lying in a darkened cave. Miss Laburnum took their temperatures and asked them if their ears hurt.

'It's very important that you keep them warm,' she told them, pulling blankets up to their robberish beards, and tucking them is so tightly that they could not toss or turn. 'But to make the time go quickly I **will read** to you. Now, what have you read already?'

These robbers had not read a thing. They were almost illiterate. 'Very well,' said Miss Laburnum, 'we **shall start** with Peter Rabbit and work our way up from there.'

Never in all their lives had those robbers been read to. In spite of the fever induced by Raging Measles they listened intently and asked for more. The robber chief listened too, though Miss Laburnum had given him the task of making nourishing broth for the invalids.

[...]

Shortly after this the robbers were quite recovered and Miss Laburnum, with her keys, went back to town. [.....] Yet, about three weeks after all these dramatic events, there was more robber trouble! Into the library, in broad daylight, burst none other than the Robber Chief.

'Save me!' he cried. 'A policeman is after me.'

Miss Laburnum gave him a cool look.

'You had better give me you full name,' she said. 'Quickly!'

The Robber Chief sprang back, an expression of horror showing through his black tangled beard.

'No, no!' he cried, 'anything but that!'

'Quickly,' repeated Miss Laburnum, 'or *I WON'T HAVE* time to help you.'

The Robber Chief leaned across the desk and whispered his name to her ... 'Salvation Loveday.'

Miss Laburnum could not help smiling a little bit. It certainly went very strangely with those wiry whiskers.

'They used to call me Sally at school,' cried the unhappy robber. 'It's that name that has driven me to a life of crime. But hide me, dear Miss Laburnum, or I **shall be caught**.'

Miss Laburnum stamped him with a number, as if he was a library book, and put him into a bookshelf with a lot of books whose authors had books beginning with L. He was in strict alphabetical order. [...]

The policeman who had been chasing the Robber chief burst into the library. [...]

'Miss Laburnum,' said the policeman, 'I have just had the occasion to pursue a notable Robber Chief into your library. I can see him there in the bookshelves among the Ls. May I take him out please?'

'Certainly!' said Miss Laburnum pleasantly. 'Do you have your library membership card?'

The policeman's face fell.

'Oh dear,' he said. 'No ... I'm afraid it's at home marking the place in my *Policemen's Robber-Catching Compendium*.'

Miss Laburnum gave a polite smile.

'I'm afraid you can't withdraw anything without your membership card,' she said. 'That Robber Chief is Library Property.'

The policeman nodded slowly. [....]

'*I'll* just *tear home* and get it,' he said. 'I don't live very far.

'Do that,' said Miss Laburnum pleasantly. [....]

Miss Laburnum went to the L shelf and took down the Robber Chief. 'Now, what are you doing here?' she said severely. However the Robber Chief was not fooled – she was really very pleased to see him.

'Well,' he replied, 'the fact is, Miss Laburnum, my men are restless. Ever since you read them those stories, they've been discontented in the evening. We used to sit around our campfire singing rombustical songs and indulging in rough humour, but they've lost their taste for it. They're wanting more *Br'er Rabbit*, more *Treasure Island*, and more stories of kings and clowns. Today I was coming to join the library and take some books out for them. What **shall I do?** I daren't go back without books, and yet that policeman may return. And WON'T HE BE angry with you when he finds I'm gone?'

'That **will be taken care of**,' said Miss Laburnum, smiling to herself. 'What is your numbers? Ah, yes. Well, when the policeman returns, I **will tell** him someone else has taken you out, and it **will be** true, for you are now issued to me.'

Teacher's reference sheet

FIVE ASPECTS TO THE FUTURE IN ENGLISH
From the text
The Librarian and the robbers

ASPECT	RULE
I *will* pay I *shall* pay	The future in English is expressed with the base of the idea-verb (i.e. the verb that is expressing what we want to say) and the auxiliary verb will or shall.
This is the **positive** aspect of the future	The *base* of the verb comes from the infinitive which in English is made up of two words e.g. *to eat, to dream, to travel*
	The *auxiliary verb* is one that helps another verb to express an aspect of thought in English: here the two auxiliary verbs *will* and *shall* help us express ourselves in the future. The term *auxiliary* comes from the Latin *auxilium* (meaning *help*) and more specifically *auxiliarius* (meaning *helpful*)
	The term *auxiliary* is also used in English in other contexts e.g. *auxiliary nurse* (a non-qualified nursing assistant) and also in the past military context: in the past there used to be *auxiliary armies*.
I will **not** pay – LONG FORM	The negative aspect of the future can be expressed in English in two ways:
I **won't** pay – SHORT FORM	• by putting **not** after the auxiliary *will/shall* • by having a shortened version **won't/shan't** which are obtained by contracting **will + not** and **shall** + not
This is the **negative** aspect of the future	
I'**ll** pay This is the SHORT form of **I will** of the **positive**	To express the future in the short form, we can put an apostrophe (') after the **I** (or any other subject/actor/agent of the main/base verb) and follow immediately with the double **ll** of *will* or *shall*
Shall I pay? Asking a **positive question** in the future	To ask a positive question in the future all we need to do is put the auxiliary verb (*will/shall*) at the beginning of the question
Won't he pay? Asking a **negative question** in the future	To ask a negative question in the future we place the negative form of the auxiliary verb (*won't/shan't*) from box 2 above at the beginning of the question

Exploring the Future and Auxiliary Verbs.
Focus Text: <u>The Great Piratical Rumbustication</u> by <u>Margaret Mahy</u>.

.Here are some ways of expressing the future in the text which I have
discovered:

• The city council <u>will</u> pay richly to have you restored. ✓

• The Cultural Committee meets in a fortnight ?

• I <u>will</u> go back to my library and borrow The Dictionary of Effluent and Efficacious Home nursing. ✓

• Of course I <u>Shall</u> only <u>be</u> able to take it out for a week. ✓

• But to make the time go quickly I <u>will</u> read to you. ✓

<u>Extra examples of the future from our class collection</u>

• If you <u>will</u> allow me

• I Shall try to alleviate the suffering of your fellows

• We'll call of the kidnapping for the present

• We <u>Shall</u> start with peter rabbit

COMPREHENSION QUESTIONS FOLLOWING THE READING OF
The Librarian and the robbers

• Who will pay richly to have Serena Laburnum, the beautiful librarian, restored? (the City Council) When? Now/Present? Yesterday/Past? Tomorrow/Future?

• Why will Miss Laburnum go to her library and borrow The Dictionary of Efficient and Efficacious Home Nursing? (to alleviate suffering) When?

• What will a hot bath do? (bring out the rash) When?

• What will Miss Laburnum read to the robbers? (Peter Rabbit) When?

• What reason does the robber give when he pleads with Miss Laburnum to hide him? ('I shall be caught') When?

• Why will the policeman be tearing home? (to get his membership card) When?

THE FUTURE and AUXILIARY VERBS OHT 1
THE FUTURE PHRASES FROM THE ADAPTED STORY

PAGE 1
....will pay....
....will meet....
....won't be....
....will allow me....
....will go....
....shall try....
....shall..be able....
....we'll call off....
....will bring out....

PAGE 2
....will read....
....shall start....
....won't have....
....shall be caught....
....I'll...tear home....
....shall I do?....
....won't he be?....
....will be taken care of....
....will tell....
....will be true....

THE NATIONAL LITERACY HOUR
THE FUTURE and AUXILIARY VERBS

LESSON ONE – 1 hour
Whole class (15 minutes)

Text level
Read the story The librarian and the robbers with the class:
Individual children take it in turns to read a short paragraph

Ask the children some general comprehension questions which will require the use of the future in the answers, e.g. who will meet in a fortnight? (paragraph 4)

After a number of questions (teacher's discretion, but six would do) to check understanding of story line, home in on the future tense i.e.

• Let's look at the words in bold – will meet (and others)

• When do you think this meeting is taking place?
Now/present, yesterday/past, tomorrow/future? Somehow elicit from the children the word future by keeping altering the question if necessary. if elicitation is unsuccesful tell the children and find other examples in the text. Teacher seeks to elicit the answer: 'Future'.

See comprehension questions below

Pair work (10 minutes)

Text level >>>>Sentence level

Hand out copies of selected pages (53-59 of referenced copy) from the original story and, working in twos, ask the children to write down on a sheet of paper (or to underline in the text, as you wish) as many sentences as they can find in the text which express the future

Ask the children to write down their own examples of sentences in the future

Whole class (15 minutes)

Text level >>>>>Sentence level

Ask some of the children to indicate the sentences they have selected and read them out while the rest of the class listens carefully in order to agree or disagree

Ask if any sentences have been missed out.

Word level

Ask the children to look only at the words will pay, shall try etcetera from OHT 1, which contains all the futures from this story.

What can they say about the words used to express the future in the story? You are eliciting the term verb from the children.

Ask the children to be more specific, read out the verbs they are referring to: e.g. in the sentence, I will go to my library, which word/s is/are the verbs?

Hopefully the children will notice that the verb go is the main verb of the sentence, which is expressing what will be happening.

Ask the children if they can see/say more specifically how the librarian expresses going in the future; i.e. which other word does she use besides go?

If the children don't come up with the word will, tell them.

Ask them if they think it's another verb; if they can't understand the concept, tell them that it is – that in English, will is another verb used together with a main verb in a sentence when we want to say something in the future. Tell the children that will/shall are auxiliary verbs which help the main verb express an idea in the future.

So if they look at the OHT 1 list, can they make up a rule for saying something in the future in English?

Elicit the future rule ASPECT 1 – see the TEACHER'S REFERENCE SHEET – from the children.

Pair work (15 minutes)

Sentence Level

Ask the children to put into the future the sentences from OHT 2; distribute copies of this sheet to the children and use the OHT as a master

Whole class (5 minutes)

Sentence level

Ask the children to read out their sentences in the future

Report back

Whole class discussion – word level

Using the list on page 128 as reference, the teacher asks the following questions to encourage pupils to talk about the verbs that make up the future.

- 'The City council will pay richly' – What can you say about these words that are used to express the future in the story?
- 'I will go to my library' – Where is the verb?
  Go is expressing what is happening
- In the last sentence, the librarian wants to get her action into the future. What words does she use besides go?
- Is will another verb? – in English: Yes, will is another verb
- Will and shall are called AUXILIARY VERBS. Auxiliary verbs help the main verb when we want to say something in the future
- Will and shall in front of a main verb help us to express the POSITIVE ASPECT of the FUTURE

LESSON TWO – 1 hour 5 minutes

Whole class (10 minutes)

Text level >>>>>>Word Level

Go back to the adapted text of The librarian and the robbers – and revise what was learnt from it in the last lesson, i.e. the construction of the future tense with auxiliary verbs; aspect 1 – the positive aspect – (see teacher's reference sheet) – was discussed; NB. Give out copies of the version with the highlighted future phrases

15 minutes

Point out to the children, one at a time, aspects 2, 3, 4, and 5 and guide a short discussion on these aspects of the future eg.

• On page 1 look at the words in capital and underlined WON'T BE

• What do they mean? Who's not going to be doing what? Does it mean something will or will not happen?

• Elicit or tell the children the negative aspect of the future

Similarly with aspect 3, the short ('ll) form of the positive

Aspect 4, asking positive questions

Aspect 5, asking negative questions

THE NATIONAL LITERACY HOUR

THE FUTURE and AUXILIARY VERBS

Pair work

LET'S PUT THESE SENTENCES FROM THE STORY

The Librarian and the robbers

INTO THE FUTURE

Present	Future
1. One day Serena Laburnum is carried off by wicked robbers	One day Serena Laburnum shall be carried off by wicked robbers
2. The robbers charge at her and carry her off	The robbers will charge at her and carry her off
3. The City Council receives a ransom note	The city council shall receive a ransom note
4. There is a lot of discussion about the kidnapping	There will be alot of discussion about the kidnapping
5. Spots are disastrous for robbers	Spots will disastrous for robbers
6. The robbers learn to enjoy listening to stories	The robbers shall learn to enjoy listening to stories
7. Three weeks later there's more trouble with the robbers	Three weeks later there shall be more trouble with the robbers
8. The Chief robber walks into the library	The chief robber will walk into the library
9. A policeman tries to catch him	A policeman shall try to catch him
10. The librarian saves him from the law	The librarian will save him from the law.

Group work (15 minutes)

Text level >>>>>>Sentence level

Give each group two group-work texts – Travel document and Churchill's speech and one grid sheet of the five aspects of the future which have been found this morning in the class-work text – see page 142.

Each group to identify aspects of the future:

- Read the text

- Find in the text any of the five aspects of the future which correspond to the grid – the text may not contain all five aspects, in which case the cell must be left blank

- Put a selected future phrase from the text into the appropriate grid

Whole class (10 minutes)

Text level>>>>>Sentence level

Review and discuss the group work investigation – all the children in each group report back quickly on the following:

> on the content of the text

> on the aspects of the future found in the text

> on aspects of the future not found in the text

> show and read out the grid as a summary of points 2 and 3

Individual work (10 minutes)

Sentence Level

Transfer newly acquired knowledge to own imagination: responding to aspect of the future in terms of the children's imagined future.

Distribute one Task sheet 3 to each child and ask them to:

> write 4 sentences about their own future, as they envisage it

> each sentence must illustrate 1 separate aspect of the five future aspects learnt in these lessons

> illustrate each sentence with a drawing

> write underneath the drawing the future aspect of that drawing's sentence

Group work text – Geography

THE BEST OF TANZANIA

Adapted from a Scott Dunn World brochure

DAY 1   You will fly overnight from London to Nairobi

Our representative will meet you at Nairobi airport and will drive you to Wilson airport where you will board a connecting flight to Kilimanjaro. A driver will be waiting for you here who will drive you directly to Maji Moto camp.

The area that you will be staying in is called Lake Manyara. Here you will visit the Lake Manyara National Park where you will enjoy dramatic views over the Rift Valley escarpment and across the lake.

DAY 4   Today you will leave Lake Manyara to travel to Ngorongoro Crater, which was once a huge active volcano – probably as large as Kilimanjaro. After its eruption its cone collapsed inwards leaving the caldera which forms a natural boundary in which there are estimated 30,000 animals.

You will stay in a lodge on the rim of the crater (you will be perfectly safe!) but you won't be allowed to venture out on your own to view the wild life. An experienced guide will accompany you through safe routes on the ancient crater.

DAY 8   You will remain here for four days and we will make sure that your stay will be very comfortable and enjoyable.

Your holiday will come to a pleasant conclusion. We hope you will take wonderful memories of your Tanzanian adventure. Our representative will collect you in the morning and will drive you back to the airport via Grumeti Camp in the north of the Serengeti. This will be your last opportunity to take in the breathtaking vistas of the beautiful East African landscape.

Whole class (5 minutes)

Sentence level

Ask some of the children to read out one sentence from their work and the corresponding grammatical explanation of the use of a particular combination of auxiliary + verb; the rest of the class listen carefully and assess. Alternatively ask the children to swap their work and assess one another's before hearing some of the sentences; collect to mark.

Group work text – History

Address to Parliament by Winston Churchill
On May 22nd 1940

'...we shall not flag or fail. We shall go on to the end... whatever the cost may be, we shall fight on the beaches, we shall fight on the landing grounds, we shall fight in the fields and in the streets, we shall fight in the hills; we shall never surrender...

But if we fail, then the whole world, including the United States, including all that we have known and cared for, will sink into the abyss of a new Dark age, made more sinister, and perhaps more protracted, by the lights of perverted science. Let us therefore brace ourselves that....men will say, 'This was their finest hour.'

Assessment

It seemed appropriate to set this sequence of lessons in the context of challenge. This is how I introduced the work to my class:

'We are going to investigate some interesting new ways of thinking about how language works in our Literacy Hour over the next few days. It is going to be rather like looking at a plan and then constructing a model, firstly seeing how the different parts fit together and then carefully taking them apart and putting them back together again, according to that plan. So our concentration has got to work really well throughout, in order that our model might work really well in the end!'

How did it all pan out?

- The character of the text provided a creative focus in itself, – in terms of investigating genre, characterisation, setting and plot, – while the comprehension questions provided a natural and effective bridge towards the preliminary process of making grammatical knowledge explicit, through a consideration of future tense, as it functioned within the text.

- The initial paired work produced much interactive discussion and interesting evidence of children beginning to 'verb search' and thereby locate specific, grammatical clues, which they could begin to differentiate from general, extended, references to the future.

THE NATIONAL LITERACY HOUR

THE FUTURE and AUXILIARY VERBS

Group work task sheet

FIVE ASPECTS TO THE FUTURE IN ENGLISH
From the group texts

GROUP'S NAME:_____

ASPECT	TEXT WHAT IS THE TEXT ABOUT?
1. I *will* pay I *shall* pay This is the **positive** aspect of the future	· you will fly overnight from London to Nairobi · Our representative will meet you at Nairobi airport and will drive you to wilson airport · A driver will be waiting for you · Here you will be visiting the Lake Manyara · Today you will leave Lake Manyara · You will stay in a lodge on the rim of the crater · You will remain here for four days · that your stay will be very comfortable · your holiday will come to a very pleasant conclusion
2. I will **not** pay – LONG FORM I **won't** pay – SHORT FORM This is the **negative** aspect of the future	· But you won't be allowed to venture out
3. I'**ll** pay This is the SHORT form of **I will** of the **positive** as in box 1.	
4. *Shall* I pay? Asking a **positive question** in the future	
5. *Won't* he pay? Asking a **negative question** in the future	

Exploring the Future and Auxiliary Verbs.
<u>The Future and ME!</u>

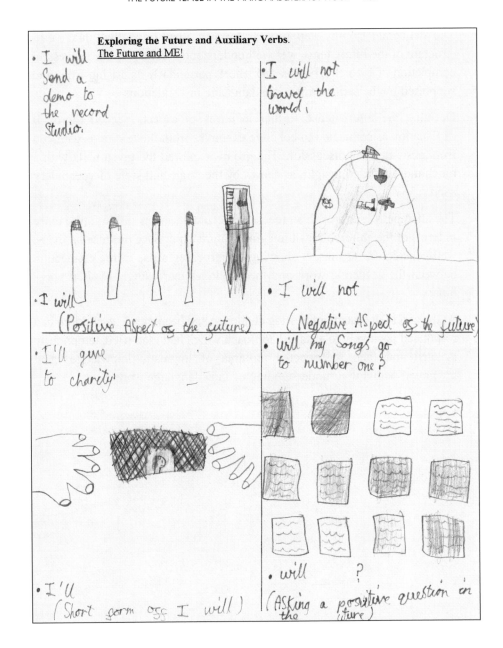

• I will
Send a
demo to
the record
studio.

• I will not
travel the
world.

• I will
___ (Positive Aspect of the future)

• I will not
___ (Negative Aspect of the future)

• I'll give
to charity!

• Will my songs go
to number one?

• I'll
(Short form of I will)

• will ?
(Asking a positive question in
the future)

- The deliberate step-by-step process towards identifying the 'dual verb' structure of the future tense was well understood – evidence: the successful completion of Into the future, task sheet, particularly as arising from and supported by the series of previous language investigations.

- Defining the future tense further in terms of aspects needed thorough explanation as connected to concrete examples from the text or as gathered from ensuing class discussion. The groups explored the given texts with a much more focused insight, as shown by the range and style of vocabulary used.

- The attempt to reinforce this process by defining aspects of the future tense in terms of the children's own imagined future experience produced a lively, well-considered, response – showing a sharpening sense of the connection between the academic work and the children's increasingly explicit vocabulary.

- At the end I felt that an interesting challenge had been met. The children had responded positively to a staged approach which had identified, temporarily isolated and then reconnected an area of linguistic knowledge, now integrated within their understanding of 'how language works'.

CHAPTER 4

THE POSSESSIVE *S* AND RELATIVE PRONOUNS

Mina Drever

The two lessons in this chapter teach what is meant by possessive s and relative pronouns. During the academic year 1996-1997 I was asked by two teachers in different schools to teach their classes two aspects of English grammar. One had a Year 4 class to whom I was to teach the idea of the possessive s. The other teacher wanted a Year 6 class to begin to learn relative pronouns. These two structures are National Curriculum requirements (NC) at KS2. The phrase relative pronoun does not appear anywhere in the 1995 National Curriculum document, nor in the National Literacy Strategy (NLS) document file. The latter has been in place since September 1998, and we consider its requirements just as we consider the NC orders. Relative pronouns are one type of pronoun, and pronouns appear in both documents. Relative pronouns are constituents of 'clauses and phrases', and are defined in both government documents as requirements for learning.

This is how these two grammatical structures are presented in the NC and NLS documents:

Possessive *s*

- NC KS2 – Key skills in punctuation, and to 'mark possession' – paragraph c page 15

- NLS – Year 4 Term 2 'to use the apostrophe accurately to mark possession' – paragraph 2 page 40

- NLS – Year 5 Term 3 – 'to revise use of apostrophes for possession' paragraph 5 page 48

Pronouns

- NC KS2 – 'to use the standard written forms of nouns, pronouns...' page 16

- NLS – Year 2 Term 2 – use 'nouns/pronouns correctly' in verb agreement, paragraph 4 page 28

- NLS – Year 3 Term 3 – 'identify pronouns and understand their functions in sentences' paragraph 2 page 36

Clauses + complex sentences

- NC KS2 – 'develop their understanding of grammar of complex sentences, including clauses and phrases' page 16

- NLS – Year 5 Term 3 – 'to investigate clauses' paragraph 6 page 48

- NLS – Year 6 Term 1 – 'to form complex sentences' paragraph 5 page 50

- NLS – Year 6 Term 2 – 'to revise work on complex sentences 'paragraph 3 page 52

- NLS – Year 6 Term 3 – 'to secure control of complex sentences, understanding how clauses can be manipulated to achieve different effects' paragraph 4 page 54

For in-depth and detailed reference I would recommend A Student's Grammar of the English language by Sidney Greenbaum and Randolph Quirk, and A Communicative Grammar of English by G. Leech and J. Svartvik (full references in the bibliography). For those with a wider interest An Introduction to Functional Grammar by M. A. K. Halliday is a detailed study of the grammatical functions of language.

Learning about relative pronouns requires a good grasp of pronouns in general and main and subordinate clauses in particular. My lesson on relative pronouns tries to ensure that pupils understand the concept of pronouns before moving on to relative pronouns. One cannot teach the clause in one lesson, or even a week, so this was not attempted. It would have been too much for anyone to cope with in one hour, let alone Year 6 pupils.

The possessive *s*

It is difficult to find this heading, – possessive s – in grammar reference books. It is more likely to be found under the heading genitive case because, in the tradition of prescriptive grammars, some linguists have retained the labels of Latin and Greek grammar, though modern English is eons removed from these ancient languages. Prescriptive grammars are so called because they prescribe how the linguistic constituents of a language fit into categories such as nouns, verbs, adjectives, etc, and how these words should be used together to construct sentences. The genitive is such a label. It denotes that something/someone can be traced back to something else or someone else in the sentence. In the English we speak today the genitive can be expressed in two ways:

- with s in the singular: eg. the boy's father; and s in the plural: eg. the boys' father

- with an of- phrase eg. the father of the boy and the father of the boys

The grammatical explanations below have been adapted from the grammar books recommended above, both of which retain the label genitive. For ease of reference I have adhered to their use of the term.

Some facts about possessive *s*

To call s a possessive s is slightly misleading because 's has a variety of meanings: (categories and examples from Greenbaum and Quirk pages 103-104)

> possessive in the sense of having eg. Mrs Johnson's coat i.e. Mrs Johnson owns this coat
>
> attribute eg. the victim's outstanding courage i.e. the victim was very courageous
>
> partitive eg. the heart's two ventricles i.e. the heart contains two ventricles
>
> subjective eg. the parents' consent i.e. the parents consented
>
> objective eg. the prisoner's release i.e. (someone) released the prisoner
>
> origin eg. mother's letter i.e. the letter is from mother
>
> descriptive eg. children's shoes i.e. the shoes are designed for children

Singular and plural possessive *s* – a few rules

(The following information and examples are derived from Svartvik, page 231)

> space 's – in the singular eg. the boy space s = the boy's shoes (the shoes of the boy)
>
> no space s' in regular plurals eg. the boys' space = the boys' shoes (the shoes of the boys)
>
> space 's – irregular plurals eg. the children space 's = the children's clothes (the clothes of the children)
>
> zero genitive i.e. no s after the apostrophe after:
>
> a)   singular nouns ending in s, eg. for goodness' sake
>
> b)   proper names ending in s, eg. Mr. Jones' or Mr. Jones's (both acceptable)
>
> c)   with Greek names eg. Euripedes' plays = the plays of Euripedes

Pronouns

A pronoun is a linguistic item used to substitute a single noun or a noun phrase. There are many different pronouns (Crystal, 1985):

- personal pronouns

I/me, we/us, you, he/him, she/her, it, they/them

*   possessive pronouns
    my/mine, our/ours, your/yours, his, her/hers, its, their/theirs

*   demonstrative pronouns
    this, that, these, those

*   interrogative pronouns
    who/whom/whose; which, what, where, when, how, whether, if (when it
    means whether)

*   reflexive pronouns
    myself, ourselves, yourself, yourselves, himself, herself, itself, themselves

*   indefinite pronouns
    everyone, everybody, each, every, all/both, no one, nobody, nothing, none,
    neither, no

*   partitive pronouns
    someone, something, somebody, a (an), some, anyone, anybody, anything,
    either, any

*   relative pronouns
    who, whom, whose, which, that and zero pronoun i.e. when it is left out
    but implied.

We are concerned with relative pronouns, the last category in the above list.
Relative pronouns are used in relative clauses. They are called relative because
they relate to something or someone that has already been mentioned. To understand the use of relative pronouns we have to understand the relative clause. A
relative clause is part of a complex sentence. The NC and NLS documents state
that children should learn to understand and use complex sentences, including
the clause and noun phrase. So our relative pronouns lesson is set in the framework of: simple and complex sentence >> clause >> relative clause.

(Examples from Quirk, page 284-370 except for 'the mouse that the cat chased'
below).

A simple sentence is one main clause, with a subject (or actor/agent), a verb and
a direct object eg.

I reject her conclusions.

I = the subject/actor/agent ; reject = verb ; her conclusions = direct object.

A complex sentence is longer and contains one main clause and any number of
subordinate clauses – subordinate meaning that it is ordered in grammatical
structural hierarchy below the main clause eg.

Although I admire her reasoning (subordinate clause)

I reject her reasoning (main clause)

A complex sentence can be complicated and even longer eg.

He predicted / 2) that he would discover the tiny particle / 3) when he conducted his next experiment

He predicted = main clause
that ....experiment = subordinate direct object clause
when ....experiment = subordinate adverbial (when) clause

There are many different types of subordinate clauses. One is the adverbial clause in the last example, introduced by the temporal adverb when. There is no scope here to discuss the others. What we must remember is that although the National Curriculum and the National Literacy Strategy documents mention bits of grammatical data which pupils should learn, language does not work in bits. In order to teach each small element, it must be placed in the wider linguistic context. Here, we will dwell on the relative clause because one of the grammar lessons in this chapter is on relative pronouns.

Relative clauses

Relative clauses can be sentential and adnominal. They are typically identified by the use of relative pronouns who, whom, that, which, whose which link the main clause and the subordinate relative clause eg.

The mouse / that the cat chased

Sentential pertains to a whole sentence, so a sentential relative clause is a subordinate clause, introduced by one of the relative pronouns, and refers back to a whole sentence before it:

Things then improved / which surprises me

An adnominal relative clause refers back to a noun phrase before it:

The taxi / that is waiting outside

Rules for using relative pronouns:

Relative pronouns can refer back to people, animals, inanimate objects, events and so on, so their use has to indicate a personal and non-personal agreement. In other words, when to say who and when to say which.

Personal relative pronouns refer to people or sometimes pets and also to collective nouns which imply a group of people, if this noun is used as a plural entity, eg. the committee who were responsible for this decision. Here who refers to the people who made up the committee. However, if the committee is thought of as an anonymous group, then we would say: the committee which was responsible for this decision. The same arguments apply to words like nation, family, government, police etc – in fact, any collective noun which implies that it is made up of people.

who: the girl who spoke to him – this who is the subject of the relative clause

whom: the girl who(m) he met – this who(m) is the object of he + verb met; one can say either who or whom in such a sentence

to whom: the girl to whom he spoke – whom is obligatory in this sentence because the verb to speak is followed by to i.e. to speak to someone (not to speak someone); so the to in front of whom is the original to of the verb

whose: this means of whom in the sense of the possessive/genitive (remember this from the possessive s?) eg. the girl, whose mother used to teach here, has failed her exams.

Non-personal relative pronouns refer to non-humans, including parts of the human body! We don't say the arm whom I broke while skiing but the arm that I broke!

which: all inanimate objects (eg. ship), animals (tigers, which are nearly extinct....), collective nouns in the singular as we have already seen (eg. committee, class, school etcetera);

that: can be used with humans and non-humans eg.

> The boy that is playing the piano
> The table that stands in the corner

Zero pronouns is just what it says: no pronoun is used in the relative clause. This is perfectly legitimate. We do it all the time, except that maybe we are not aware that we are using zero pronouns!

> The boy we met = the boy who(m) / that we met
> The table we admire = the table which we admire

LESSON
THE POSSESSIVE s

Class: Year 4
Number of pupils: 21

Differentiated groups: Group 1 – Level 1 or working > towards 1 in English
(for this lesson)   Group 2 – Level 1>2
                         Group 3 – Level 3 > 4

These were the levels of attainment of the groups in the National Curriculum assessment at the time of this lesson. The differentiated tasks were designed so that the level of linguistic demand was equal to the NC levels attained by the children. These tasks were discussed with the class teacher to ensure that I had gauged it right.

Term's topic: Poetry
Poem selected for this lesson: Eddie in Bed by Michael Rosen

Approach to grammar teaching
• content-based, drawn from NC and school curriculum.

• eliciting rules of grammar from children by focusing on and emphasising the structure ('s) in modelled known context.

Time allocated: 1$\frac{1}{2}$ hours
It would be usual for a grammar lesson to be no longer than 30-40 minutes for this age group. However, as this was in a sense a demonstration lesson, I wanted to show as much as possible how they could learn new grammatical structures, starting with a text they knew and liked, and then transfer this new grammatical knowledge to real life knowledge.

Materials
• photocopies of the poem Eddie in Bed – one copy per child

• nine illustration cards used during the oral comprehension work on the poem during session 2 of the lesson structure; these drawings illustrate different relationships in the poem, eg. Eddie's mum

• differentiated task sheets for three groups:

        Group L1/2 – task sheet 1

        Group L2 – task sheet 2

        Group L3/4 – task sheet 3

• one A3 size master sheet of task sheets 1, 2, 3 for the whole class reporting back session 3 in the lesson structure

• listening text for focused listening – in this lesson this text was read to the whole class but it can be used with small groups, pairs or individuals and can be recorded for small group or individual activities (recording would be a distinct advantage for individuals/pairs because it could be played back as often as the children need)

- listening task sheets for whole class work on focused listening

- one A3 size master sheet of the listening task for the reporting back session 5 of the lesson structure

- five illustration cards for extension oral work

- task sheets for the three differentiated groups to extend this new grammatical concept from familiar learning context (the poem) to personal life experiences:

> Group L1/ 2 – task sheet 4
>
> Group L2 – task sheet 5
>
> Group L3/4 – task sheet 6

LESSON STRUCTURE
THE POSSESSIVE 'S

Session 1 (whole class) Oral work – teacher-directed

- read the poem with the class – ask different children to read a few lines

- ascertain that pupils understanding the characters (who's who) in the poem and their roles/relationships (see question sheet)

- as children give correct answers, put these up against the wall, the illustration cards 1-9, one at a time, i.e. each card goes with a particular question/ answer. NB each card's phrase highlights the possessive 's in colour. Highlighting makes discussion more straightforward and focuses the children's attention

Discussion – teacher-directed

All the cards are now on the wall and children can see the illustrated roles/ relationships in the poem and direct the discussion along these lines:

- look at the writing beneath the drawings on the cards – what do you see? Elicit coloured 's

- does anyone know/can guess why it's there? Elicit belonging to

- focus on card 1: whose name is it? Yours/mine/hers? NO, it is EDDIE'S name, therefore the name of Eddie belongs to the baby and we say that the baby's name is Eddie

CONTINUE WITH THE REST OF THE CARDS IN THIS WAY

Session 2 (Group activities) three differentiated group tasks

There were three teachers in class during this lesson so they explained the different tasks like this:

- each teacher responsible for one group explains the task to the group. The rest of the class does not know what the other groups' tasks involve – this is because we wanted each group to explain to the other groups what it had been doing, at the reporting-back part of this session. For teachers working on their own, it is possible to involve children in this way too: explain the three tasks to the class and ask the groups to say in their own words what they did at the reporting back session, as a way of reminding the other groups

  - groups show their work to the rest of the class in this way:

  - on the board stick A3 size master sheets of each group's task sheet

  - ask one member of each group to come and complete one phrase on the master sheet as it has been done on the group's sheet

  - this child to ask the other pupils what they think of the phrase just completed: is it right or wrong?

Session 3 (whole class) Focused listening – one short-answers task sheet for everyone

The listening text has been adapted from the poem Eddie in Bed

- read the text to the class

- distribute the task sheets and explain what to do

- read the text again and pupils look at the task sheet: they may start this task now, but they don't have too

- read the text again: this time ask the children to complete the task

- if it's necessary, repeat the last step: the children could be asked if they want to repeat this step – it's not a test, just a learning/reinforcement activity

- put an A3 master sheet of this task onto the board

- ask some pupils to come and complete the sheet (one line per child) on the board

- this child to ask for agreement from the rest of the class eg. did you do the same as this? Do you agree with me?

THIS POINT MAY MARK THE END OF ONE LESSON AND WHAT FOLLOWS OCCUPY A SECOND LESSON. WE CONTINUED IN ONE LONG LESSON.

Session 4 (whole class) Oral – teacher-led discussion – Extend/relate the concept of 's to personal belongings/ relations – use cards 10-14

- ask a pupil: do you have a coat? What colour is it?

- Stick card 1 on the board and write next to it: '_____ coat is_____ '

- Repeat this little activity with all the cards, asking a different pupil for each card: card 4 +brother/sister and name; card 2 + television + size; card 5 + pet + type; card 3 + soft toy + its name/colour/age

Session 5 (Group work)
Differentiated task sheets to each group

> Group L1/2 – task sheet 4
> Group L2 – task sheet 5
> Group L3/4 – task sheet 6

This session to be carried out along the same lines and principles as the last group session: teachers explain the tasks and supervise the task activities; groups report back as before

TIMING

No timing has been put on these sessions. Group sessions lasted five minutes each on task. This was sufficient because the tasks are very short: longer tasks would obviously require more time. So although timing must be strict, as in all our lessons, it will depend on the amount and degree of complexity of the task.

FOLLOW-UP WORK

This would have to be the plural of the possessive s, e.g.

> The boys' father = the father of the boys

The learning of possessive s is not complete unless both singular and plural conventions are considered.

THE POSSESSIVE S
UNDERSTANDING A POEM – QUESTIONS FOR SESSION 1

Questions	Answer
Who looks really tired?	Eddie's father
What can he hear?	The baby's screams
What's the baby's name?	Eddie
Where is Eddie sitting up?	In his bed
Who has nightmares	Eddie
Why is he screaming?	He wants biscuits
Where is Eddie sleeping?	In his brother's bed
What's his brother's name?	Joe
Where is Joe's head?	Next to Eddie's hips
Who wants to know what's going on?	Joe
Where does Eddie go?	His parents' bed
Who is Susanna?	Eddie's mum
Where is Eddie's head now?	Next to Susanna's head
And his feet?	In his father's ear
What does his father do in the morning?	Change Eddie's nappy

EDDIE IN BED

Sometimes I look really tired,
because you see
when most people are fast asleep
and I'm fast asleep
I hear,
"waaaaaaaaaaaaaaaaaaaaaaa."
That's the baby, Eddie.
So I get out of bed and go into his room
and he's sitting up in bed
and he has these nightmares.
Not nightmares like you have,
like Dracula biting your head off or something.
He has nightmares about people taking food away from him.
So one night I go in there
and he's sitting up in bed
lifting his arms above his head
and banging them down
screaming,
"I want my biscuits I want my biscuits."

Now if you can imagine that,
you can also imagine
that at this time he was sleeping
in the same bed as his brother.
Who was six.
And you have to imagine his brother's head
is right next to Eddie's hip.
Think about it.
Eddie's hands go above his head and
Wham
down by his side
right on Joe's nut.
"I want my biscuits I want my biscuits."
So Joe lifts his head and he goes,
"What's going on?"
Wham
"I want my biscuits."
"What's going on?"

Wham
"I want my biscuits."
"What's going on?"
Wham
"I want my biscuits."
"Stop it, Eddie" – wham back
"I want my biscuits."
Wham.
"OK, fellas," I say,
"Cut it out."
And I lift Eddie up and I take him into our bed.

What a stupid thing to do.

You see
most people sleep with their head
on the pillow
and their feet at the other end of the bed.
When Eddie comes into our bed
he sleeps with his head next to Susanna's head
and his feet in my ear.

And you have to imagine those feet
sticking in my ear.
And the toes.
Those toes are going
wiggle wiggly wiggly
Down my ear.
All night.
So by the time I get up
in the morning
I'm very tired
and very cross.

But I can always get my own back on him
in the morning
cos he hates having his nappy done ...

the baby's name
is
Eddie

Eddie's father

Eddie's
screams

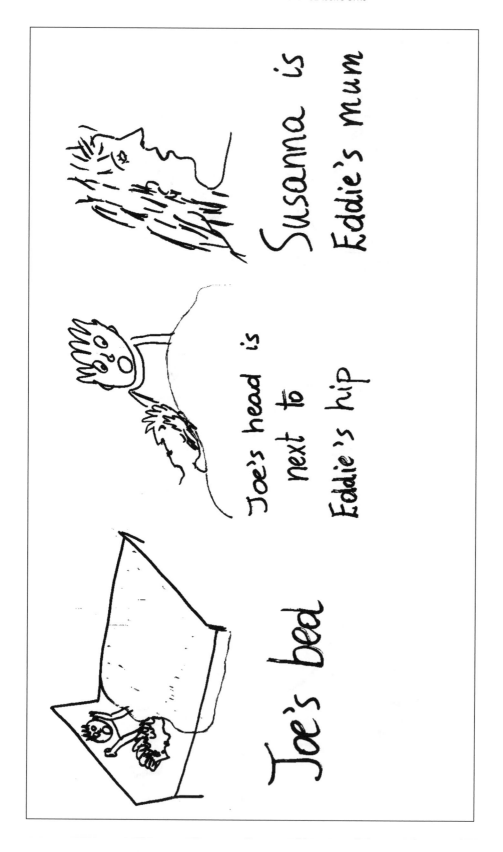

Put these words together so that they show which one belongs to the other one.

You need to put 's.

example: *Eddie*   –   *the baby / name*

                                the baby's name

1.      Joe / bed

2.      Eddie / biscuits

3.      Eddie / screams

4.      mother / head

5.   father / ear

Write a little phrase to describe the drawings. Look at the example carefully.

example:

Eddie's screams

1.

2.

3.

4.

5.

SESSION 2 – TASK SHEET 3 – GROUP L3/4

Read the poem Eddie in bed.

Complete these sentences with any number of words which make sense.

Remember 's.

Each line needs one word.

Father hears _____ _____ screams.

Eddie is sleeping in _____ _____ bedroom.

His _____ name is Joe.

His _____ name is Susanna.

Father takes Eddie to his own bed. Eddie lies with his head next to _____ _____ head and his feet in _____ _____ ear.

Can you think of some sentences of your own which you can make up from the poem? Write them here.

Example: Eddie's biscuits are in the kitchen.

THE POSSESSIVE *S*

SESSION 3 – THE LISTENING TEXT

Our baby is a pain. Eddie, that is our baby's name. Every night, just as I am about to fall asleep, what do you think I hear? The telephone? Or is it the door bell? Maybe the alarm clock? Oh no! Always his loud piercing screams.

Finally I get up and go to Joe's bedroom. There I find the little rascal bouncing up and down and pulling his brother's hair. 'Ouch! Take him away! Please! Ouch! Hell! Take him away!' begs Joe. So, into our bed he comes. Do you think I get any sleep? No such luck! He stretches out, with his feet in my ear, and I am finally pushed off onto the floor.

SESSION 4 – WHOLE CLASS

Listening task sheet

Listen carefully to this very short story. When you hear the clue words written above the boxes, tick *one* box only.

1. Father hears...........?

2. Father goes into...........?

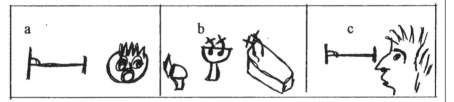

3. Eddie pulls whose hair?

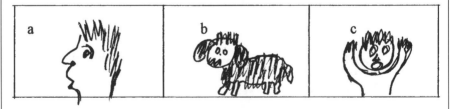

4. Eddie stretches out onto..............?

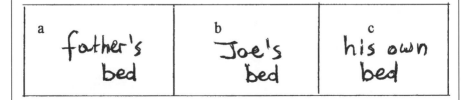

THE POSSESSIVE S
SESSION 5 – TASK SHEET 4 – GROUP 1/2

Draw some pictures to go with these sentences.
Colour them if you wish.

example: *The flower's petals are yellow*.

1. The candle's flame is red.

2. This tree's leaves are round.

3. My dog's tail is long and thin.

4. The table's legs are broken.

Write a phrase for each drawing.

example: *The window's curtains.*

1.

2.

3.

4.

THE POSSESSIVE *S*
SESSION 5 – TASK SHEET 5 – GROUP L2

Put the words from column *a* together with those in columns *b* and *c* to create a sentence.

example:	*a*	*b*	*c*
	this boy	*name*	*Peter*
	This boy's name is Peter.		

	a	b	c
1.	Eddie	brother	sensible
	_____		
2.	Your pen	colour	green
	_____		
3.	Rachel	nose	straight
	_____		
4.	My mother	eyes	dark brown
	_____		

Now make some sentences for these drawings. Choose yourr own words. Remember *'s*.

example: The ship's sail is up.

1.

2.

3.

4.

THE POSSESSIVE S
SESSION FIVE – TASK SHEET 6 – GROUP L3/4

Change the a) sentences into b) sentences as in the example.
Remember 's.

Example:　　　　The handle of this door is sticky

　　　　　　　　This door's handle is sticky

The mother of Raoul is a doctor.

_____

Lucinda has straight hair.

_____

The head of our school is Mrs Clever.

_____

Mrs Efficient has a black briefcase.

_____.

Now you need to do the opposite. Change the a) sentences by taking away the 's:
you'll get b) type sentences as in the example.

Example:　　　　The sun's rays are very hot.

　　　　　　　　The rays of the sun are very hot.

Rosheen's brother speaks two languages.

_____

Our school's gate are made of iron.

_____

I like Michael Rosen's poems.

_____

RELATIVE PRONOUNS

This was a Year 6 class of 29 pupils. The class's teacher was particularly concerned about the generally poor use of relative pronouns. There was a whole-class teaching ethos, so the children were used to participating in whole-class discussions.

Aim:

to introduce the class to the concept of relativisation and the pronouns which express it.

Objectives:

*   learn what a pronoun is; identify pronouns, use pronouns verbally and in writing

*   learn what a relative pronoun is; identify relative pronouns; use relative pronouns verbally and in writing

Approach:

Present these grammatical forms and structures in meaningful contexts which will capture the pupils' attention

Materials:

*   own shortened version of Red Riding Hood

*   adapted story Why the jaguars can see in the dark (from the book Just How Stories – by Girls of Lady Eden's School, London; published by Jonathan Cape, London, 1981)

*   nursery rhyme, This is the house that Jack built, from Popular Nursery Rhymes, (edited by J. Mulherin, published by Granada, London,1981)

*   ten activity sheets for a mixture of whole class oral discussions and written tasks in pairs

*   overhead projector and transparencies of all task sheets

*   posters made for a wall display

Lesson Structure

This lesson was very long and was not completed. This had been envisaged and the class teacher and I decided that I should prepare a sequence of learning units which would naturally follow from one another. I was to introduce the class to the idea of relativisation and the rest of the work would be completed at another time. We got as far as reading the jaguar's story together.

The teacher observed at the end of the lesson that the materials prepared are quite simple and the activities focus on basic phrases and sentence construction, which could have been a little insulting for a Year 6 class. However, we noticed that

- the children enjoyed the materials and activities; the contextual familiarity and the simplicity of the tasks enabled them to focus on the new linguistic concept and metalanguage

- though the tasks were simple, some children were struggling in the initial stages with the grammatical notion of relative pronouns. This indicated to the teacher that maybe a global approach to language teaching (the normal school approach) might pass many children by and a more local focus (as in this lesson) could be more conducive to learning about language.

Session 1 Oral discussion
(whole class) 10 minutes
Task sheet 1 as transparency on OHP or one copy per child

- Place transparency on OHP and invite children to read the content i.e. the pronouns, the instructions, then one sentence at a time

- ask children to explain choice of pronouns: 'Why did you say she for grandma?' Elicit 'because she's female' or similar

- guide the conversation towards noun/pronoun using this OHT/task sheet: e.g.

- what sort of a word is Red Riding Hood? >>> proper name

- what other proper names can you think of? >>> people/countries

- what sort of a word is flower? >>> naming noun (common nouns)

- can you see any other nouns that are not proper nouns? eg. grandma, door, wolf, wood cutter, home

- what about she, it, you, them, they, her, him, he: are these nouns?

- elicit no!

- tell the children that these are called pronouns and are used instead of, in substitution for nouns (pro meaning in place of/for)

- show the children OHT 2: see whether they can see the connection between the pronouns and the drawings; elicit that it is used for non-people, them for all plurals, he/him for singular males, she/her for singular females

Session 2 Pronouns – written task
(pair work) 5 minutes

- distribute task sheet 4, one per child

- Put OHT 3 on the OHP and cover the relative pronouns half; let the children use the Pronouns list to complete the cloze task 4

- pairs to contribute to reporting back which pronouns have gone where: put OHT of task sheet 4 on OHP and write in children's selected pronouns as they read them out

- ask the rest of the class to judge the whether the choice made is correct and/or make different suggestions

Session 3 Relative pronouns
(whole class) 10 minutes
Task sheet 5 and OHT
How to make two sentences into one by using *who/that/which*

- ask one child to read out the instruction

- ask another child to read out the example sentences

- discuss the examples: what has been done; how many sentences in a)? how many in b)? what is the difference? Elicit observations on punctuation changes and the insertion of who in b)

- do sentences 1, 2 and 3 together as a class, inviting different children to attempt them orally and seeking whole class agreement

(pair work) 5 minutes

- distribute task sheet 5

- ask children, in pairs, to rewrite sentences 4, 5, 6, 7

(whole class) 5 minutes

- Pairs to read out their changed sentences and the rest of the class to judge them

- discuss any differences to pupils' choices between the relative pronouns – this leads easily into the next discussion

Session 4 Relative pronouns and relations –
oral discussion – blank OHT or the board
(whole class) 10 minutes

- ask some children names/ages/professions of relatives eg. 'Have you an uncle'?

- child replies 'Yes I have an uncle'

- write on the OHT/board 'I have an uncle'

- ask 'What's your uncle's name?' – reply: 'His name is Tom'

- write on the OHT / board 'My uncle is called Tom'

- write a new sentence on OHT / board 'I have an uncle who is called Tom'

- Continue like this for three more examples

(pair work) 5 minutes
- ask children to write as many sentences as 'I have an uncle who ..' in 5 minutes

(whole class) 5 minutes
Pairs to read out their sentences and rest of the class to judge them

Session 5 Oral discussion – OHT 6 and OHT 7
(whole class) 5 minutes
- with OHT 6 explain to the children the personal/non-personal relationships of the relative pronouns

- with OHT 7 ask individual children to try and complete a sentence as example to the whole class

(pair work) 5 minutes
- written task sheet 8

- individual children to read out a sentence from task sheet 8

- rest of the class to judge them correct or not and suggest alternatives

What came next could be a follow-up lesson at some other time. This is consolidation learning – making sure that learning has taken place. Also, we are using published texts – children can see here that relative pronouns, like verbs, are part and parcel of everybody's linguistic repertoire

Session 6 Focused listening
– adapted story: Why the jaguar can see in the dark
(whole class) 20 minutes

- show OHT 8 to the class: discuss what the story might be about; anticipate with the class any new vocabulary they might hear in the story: eg. jungle, jaguar, creature, mane, fascinate, flamingo, sparks

- distribute task sheets 9 and ask the children to leave them face down

- ask pupils to carry on looking at the picture of the jaguar while listening to the first reading of the story; tell them that there are relative pronouns in the story – who, which, that – and to listen out for them

- after the first reading ask them to turn over task sheet 9; look at it together to make sure they understand what to do

- ask the children to complete this task during this second reading

- ask individual students to read out their completed sentences and the rest of the class to agree/disagree

Session 7
Model reading >> creative writing – text:
This is the house that Jack built
(whole class) 10-15 minutes

- read the first five verses of the rhyme

- look at verse 5 and answer comprehension questions eg. who/what worried the cat? Who(m) did the cat kill? Who built the house?

- ask children to explain their answers by pointing out the relative pronoun which gives them the correct answer

- on a blank OHT write: this is the flower that Rona found (see task 10)

- as a class construct two/three other lines around it e.g. this is the vase that held the flower that Rona found (see task sheet 10)

Group work 15 minutes

- allocate a different rhyme to be written in groups of four, starting with a given line (Task sheet 10) – as much as can be written in 10 minutes

- each group to read out own verse

OHT 1 or Task sheet 1 – Session 1 – Whole class Discussion

He	she	it
Him	her	they
You	them	

Read the a) sentences carefully: some words are underlined.

In the b) sentences replace the underlined words in a) with one of the words in the box.

Example:

Red Riding Hood picked some flowers

She took them to her granny

a) The wolf came to the door.
b) _____ opened _____quickly.

a) Grandma spoke to the wolf.
b) _____ told _____ to come closer.

a) The wood cutter chased the wolf.
b) '_____ are done for!!', _____ shouted.

a) Red Riding Hood hugged grandma.
b) _____ gave _____ the flowers.

a) Red Riding Hood and grandma went home.
b) _____ lived happily ever after.

Session 2 – Pair Work – OHT 3
To be used with Task Sheet 4

PRONOUNS	RELATIVE PRONOUNS
He	Who
She	Whom
It	Whose
You	Which
Him	That
Her	
They	
Them	

TASK SHEET 4 – PAIR WORK

Put a pronoun in the blank spaces. The pronoun must make sense with the words around it.

Red Riding Hood lived with her mother in a country cottage. _____ were very happy together. One day _____ asked her mother if _____ could visit grandma, who lived very near, on the other side of the wood. '_____ must promise me to be very careful', said her mother. 'I've heard that there's a nasty wolf around. I have never seen _____ but _____ has been spotted by your cousins. Here, I have baked this cake. Take _____ to grandma and give _____ my love.'

On the way the young girl saw some beautiful flowers and stopped to pick _____. When, later, she came upon the big bad wolf, she did not recognise _____ at all.

SESSION ONE – WHOLE CLASS DISCUSSION – OHT 2

Session Three – Task Sheet 5 – whole class discussion and written pair work

Turn these two sentences into one by using either who / that / or which

Example:
A young girl liked going to the woods. She was called Red Riding Hood.
A young girl, who was called Red Riding Hood, liked going to the woods.

I have just read a story. It is called Red Riding Hood.

The girl's mother baked a cake. The cake was absolutely delicious.

The child picked some flowers. They smelled heavenly.

Grandma heard a knock. The knock was loud and insistent.

There was a dangerous wolf in the area. He liked to roam in the woods at night.

Red Riding Hood heard a voice. The voice sounded just like grandma's.

I will now finish this story. It has bored me dreadfully.

Session Six – Focused listening – reading text

WHY THE JAGUAR CAN SEE IN THE DARK

A long time ago, there lived a jaguar who could not see in the dark. This made him very angry, so he went to his friend the frog, who told him: 'Take two pieces of wood and rub them together very hard. See what happens. The jaguar, who was called Onza, found two pieces of wood that he rubbed and rubbed together, until .... they made a big flame. Every bird and creature that lived in the jungle came to see this wonderful sight. Onza was so pleased with himself that he started dancing around the fire.

'Be careful', cried the frog, 'you might burn your lovely mane'. But it was too late. The jaguar's lovely mane, which had already burnt, had black spots on it now. The butterflies, which tried to comfort him, said: 'Now your mane is like our wings'. But Onza did not like having black spots. He stared and stared into the flames. The frog said: 'Don't stare at the fire too much, which is so bad for your eyes!'.

Onza did not hear the frog. He kept staring into the fire, which so fascinated him. He stared and stared until he could see circles floating around. Nobody knew what to do with Onza, who was very unhappy now. At last the parrot had an idea. He flew to the magic pond that the flamingo guarded and asked the flamingo to bring some water that was so precious. When they returned to Onza, they put three drops into each eye, which made Onza see again. But the magic waters never washed away the little sparks that remained in his eyes, so to this day all jaguars can see in the dark.

SESSION FIVE – TASK SHEET 8 – PAIR WORK

CLASSROOM ACTIVITY - TASK SHEET - PAIR/INDIVIDUAL

that?   *who?*   *which?*

**complete these sentences: name the drawing and choose
a relative pronoun to go with it**

_____, _____ you are reading, is my favourite.

_____ is a country _____ I would like to visit.

Mr. Gibson, _____ is our headteacher, is a very kind man.

_____, _____ has just crossed the road, lives next

door to me.

Session Six – Individual Listening – Task Sheet 9

Who   which   that

Listen to the reading. Put one of these relative pronouns on the blank line. You must use the one that you hear in the story.

'... a jaguar _____ could not see in the dark'

'... the frog _____ told him'

'... bird and creature _____ lived in the jungle'

'... butterflies _____ tried to comfort him'

' ... the fire _____ fascinated him'

'... pond _____ the flamingo guarded'

Session Seven – Creative Group Work – Task Sheet 11

Each group to produce a rhyming poem beginning with the given lines and using the pronoun given.

... that ...
this is the cat that sat on the mat

... which ...
here is a stone which lay on the bed

... who ...
here is the girl who wrote the poem

... that ...
this is a scarf that used to be red

... who ...
this is the angel who fell from the sky

SESSION SEVEN – CLASS DISCUSSION >>
CREATIVE WRITING
TEXT FOR DISCUSSION – OHT 9

THIS IS THE HOUSE THAT JACK BUILT

THIS IS THE HOUSE THAT JACK BUILT

This is the house that Jack built.

This is the malt
That lay in the house that Jack built.

This is the rat
That ate the malt
That lay in the house that Jack built.

This is the cat
That killed the rat,
That ate the malt
That lay in the house that Jack built.

This is the dog,
That worried the cat,
That killed the rat,
That ate the malt
That lay in the house that Jack built.

CLASSROOM ACTIVITY - ORAL

that?   *who?*   *which?*

let's name the drawing and choose a relative pronoun
to go with it

_____, _____ is swimming, is my friend Raoul.

_____, _____ contains a hat,

is round.

_____, _____ I prepared for you, has brandy

in it.

relative

pronouns

which / that

animals

who/

that

people

which / that

events

objects

CHAPTER 5
CONCLUSION

We have been guided in our approach to teaching English to primary school children by the principle that language is never fully in place, neither is it linear. (Karmiloff-Smith, 1985; O'Donnell et al, 1967), and that explicit instruction must be better than no instruction (MacWhinney, 1977). The authors of this book have found that there is much language that children have difficulty with, especially in producing complex sentences. Control of syntax in children should be characterised by a wide range of structures, increased use of sentence-combining transformations, and increased use of main clauses and subordinate clauses (O'Donnell et al, 1967). Yet investigations uncovered a most interesting paradox, namely that 'kindergarten children used relative clauses more frequently than did children at any other stage in either speech or writing' (ibid. p.60). It could be that children are not capable of deducing the rules of language from text presentation (Gold, 1967). This learning theory posited that children work out the rules for sentence construction by themselves, even though they received no correction when they made production errors. We have seen evidence that this may not be the case – that children do indeed receive instruction and feedback, no matter how implicit. Their linguistic prowess may have more to do with the brain's capacity to sift out the information needed for a particular linguistic transaction at a particular time, using particular linguistic symbols (Deacon, 1997; Ochs and Schieffelin, 1995), than with the ability to analyse how linguistic constructions are arrived at.

During middle childhood children develop the ability to make grammatical judgements but are unable to explain why a sentence is, in their opinion, acceptable or not (Hakes, 1980; Pratt and Grieve, 1984). Children have especial difficulty with understanding written text. Reading can display a 'fluency which belies their comprehension' (Wishart, 1987 p 31). Conjunction can present the greatest difficulty and substitution is poorly understood (ibid). Even at the upper end of primary school children have difficulty with anaphoric linguistic items, i.e. pronouns which refer to someone or something already mentioned in the text – I, me, you, they and so on (Hadley, 1987). Perera (1984) gives a comprehensive review of the difficulties primary school children encounter with interpretation of written text. Children in Perera's investigations appear to have difficulty especially at the sentence level, possibly because some structures are acquired late by children (p.288-302), for example complex sentences which contain a main clause and any number of subordinate clauses, like relative clauses. Another compounding factor in text interpretation could be that some structures are difficult to segment (ibid. p.302-314) into comprehensible units. This is because, unlike speech, written text does not provide the reader with acoustic cues like intonation and pitch which mark boundaries between phrases and sentences. This reliance on stress in speech may be sufficient for understanding complex sentences, but these may be just too difficult to produce them (Hornby, 1971).

There could be difficulties intrinsic to the semantics of language. We have seen in our own classrooms (see chapters 2 and 3) that children have a limited understanding of the semantic uses of certain lexical items, like 'feeling' and 'stage'. We suggested in chapter 1 that semantics and syntactic structure are closely related. The meanings we attribute to certain words and the way they are used in sentences may affect the interpretation we attach to the sentence as a whole. For example, certain adjectives present particular difficulties. Take the sentence 'Children are nice to understand' (Cromer, 1970). Who is doing the understanding? The children or someone else? To unravel this sentence, children would need to be aware that it (as all sentences in English) has a surface structure, i.e. the words as they are uttered and written, the sentence as it is heard and written. So, 'Children are nice to understand' is the surface (what you see is what you get!) structure of this string of words. Underlying this sentence construction is a deep structure (Chomsky, 1957, 1965), in a sense the source of this sentence. For example, this sentence could derive from:

• we find it nice to understand children – i.e. it gives us a sense of reward, it makes us feel good if we do the understanding of what children say and do;

or

• it is nice of children to understand – i.e. children understand when there is a problem, they are gracious about it and that's nice of them.

Ambiguity, says Cromer, lies with the adjective 'nice', which is ambiguous and can be used to refer to different subjects or agents in a sentence. The deep structure and the surface structure of a sentence may have the same subject or different subject. If the two structures have the same subject, there is no problem with understanding it straight away: for example a sentence like 'He is glad to be here' is completely clear. There are no doubts that it is 'he' who is glad and nobody else. If we try to turn this surface structure into a deep structure we'd find that they are the same. There cannot be anyone else implicated, at any level of grammatical structure, in the 'being glad'. So this is a sentence which children would find no difficulty understanding. Our sentences a) and b) above have different subjects: 'we' in a) and 'the children' in b). If the original sentence – 'Children are nice to understand' originates in b), then there is no problem with comprehension. If, however its source, lies in a), confusion may arise. Children would have to refer to other distant clues in the text and other grammatical knowledge for their accurate interpretation of what they are reading.

We are not suggesting teaching such complicated theoretical linguistic concepts to children. They are hard enough for linguists themselves! The point is that there could be difficulties within the language which are stopping children from understanding what they hear and read, and from producing complex constructions themselves. If we accept and go along with the nativists' position that language will develop regardless of the input and feedback children receive, we would be better off leaving it alone. If, on the other hand, we agree that children are not born with 'grammatical patterns' (Ochs and Schieffelin, 1995 p73) in their brains, then we may choose to assist the development of children's grammatical socialisation (ibid.). In the classrooms described in this book, we aim to help children to develop a sensitivity to the 'indexical' (ibid. p74) use of grammatical forms. By this we mean that children may learn to make associations between the grammatical forms and the cultural meanings they symbolise and represent, because

> In every community, grammatical forms are inextricably tied to, and hence index, culturally organised situations of use and the indexical meanings of grammatical forms influence children's production and understanding of these forms. (ibid. p74)

To assist children towards this grammatical acculturation we have devised two frameworks for teaching English: collaborative learning and explicit grammatical instruction. The two approaches complement each other, as in chapters 2 and 3, where collaborative learning is incorporated into explicit grammatical learning and explicit instructions are part and parcel of the collaborative writing projects. What is unique about these approaches is that they consist of intentional interventions in children's language development. There is empirical evidence to suggest that language skills may develop faster and better with instructional intervention than without it. We do this in our classrooms by constructing very tight learning parameters:

In collaborative learning we

- focus on the linguistic goal
- train pupils on collaborative ethics

- organise children's learning behaviours
- establish high expectations

In explicit grammar teaching we

- identify a language structure
- place it in the wider linguistic frame

- present it in familiar and meaningful contexts
- analyse its metalinguistic properties

Both frameworks involve

- children's interactive participation
- a cross-curricular perspective
- skill transference
- discussion, exploration, reflection
- time and practice
- whole-class teaching
- group/pair/individual activities
- a balance between these teaching approaches.

Bibliography

Anderson, J R (1982) Acquisition of Cognitive Skill, Psychological Review, 89(4) 369-406

Baker, N D and Nelson, K E (1984) Recasting and Related Conversational Techniques for Triggering Syntactic Advances by Young Children, in K Durkin and S Rogers (eds) First Language. Volume 5, 3-22. Chalfont St Giles: Alpha Academic

Berko Gleason, J (1997) The Development of Language. Boston: Allyn and Bacon

Bernstein, B (1975) Class, Codes and Control. Volume 3. Towards a Theory of Educational Transmission, London: Routledge and Kegan Paul

Biott, C and Easen, P (1994) Collaborative Learning in Staffrooms and Classrooms. London: David Fulton

Bowey, J A and Tunmer, W E (1984) Word Awareness in Children. In W E Tunmer, C Pratt and M L Herriman (eds) Metalinguistic Awareness in Children: theory, research and Implications 73-91. Berlin: Springer-Verlag

Bohannon III, J N and Bonvillian, J D (1997) Theoretical Approaches to Language Acquisition. In J Berko Gleason (ed) The Development of Language. Boston: Allyn and Bacon

Bohannon III, J N and Stanowicz, L (1988) The Issue of Negative Evidence: Adult Responses to Children's Language Errors, Developmental Psychology, 24(5), 684-689

Braine, M D S (1971) On Two types of Models of the Internalisation of Grammar. In D I Slobin, The Ontogenesis of Grammar, New York: Academic Press

Braine, M D S (1994) Is Nativism Sufficient? Journal of Child Language, 21(1), 9-31

Brown, R (1973) A First Language. The Early Stages. Cambridge, Massachusetts: Harvard University Press

Brown, R and Bellugi, U (1964) Three Processes in the Child's Acquisition of Syntax. Harvard Educational Review, 34(2), 133-151

Burgess, A (1992) A Mouthful of Air. Language and Languages. Especially English. London: Vintage

Carroll, S and Swain, M (1993) Explicit and Implicit Negative Feedback. An Empirical Study of the Learning of Linguistic Generalisations, Studies in Second Language Acquisition 15(3), 357-386

Chomsky, N (1957) Syntactic Structures. The Hague: Mouton Publishers

Chomsky, N (1965) Aspects of the Theory of Syntax. Cambridge, Massachusetts: The MIT Press

Chomsky, N (1988) Language and Problems of Knowledge. The Managua Lectures. Cambridge, Massachusetts: The MIT Press

Cole, K N, Dale, P S and Mills, P E (1990) Defining Language Delay in Young Children by Cognitive Referencing: Are We Saying More Than We Know? Applied Psycholinguistics, 11, 291-302

Cromer, R F (1970) Children are nice to understand: surface structure clue for the recovery of a deep grammar, The British Journal of Psychology, 61, 397-408

Cromer, R F (1976) The Cognitive Hypothesis of Language Acquisition and its Implications for

Child Language Deficiency, in D Morehead and A Morehead (eds) Normal and Deficient Child Language. Baltimore: University Park Press

Cromer R F (1988) The Cognition Hypothesis Revisited, in F S Kessel (ed) The Development of Language and Language Researchers. Hillsdale, NJ: Erlbaum

Cross, T G (1978) Mothers' Speech and its Association with Rate of Linguistic Development in Young Children, in N Waterson and C Snow (eds) The Development of Communication, 199-216. Chichester: John Wiley and Sons

Crystal, D (1985) A Dictionary of Linguistics and Phonetics Oxford: Basil Blackwell

Cummins, J and Swain, M (1986) Bilingualism in Education. London: Longman

D'Ascoli, F (1993) Nuovo Vocabolario Dialettale Napoletano. Repertorio Completo delle Voci. Approfondimenti Etimologici. Fonti Letterarie. Locuzioni Tipiche. Napoli: Adriana Gallina Editore

Davidson, N (1994) Cooperative and Collaborative Learning in J. S. Thousand, R. A. Villa and A. I. Nevin (eds) Creativity and Collaborative Learning 13-30. Baltimore: Paul H. Brookes Publishing Co

Davies, W D and Kaplan, T I (1998) Native Speakers vs. L2 Learner Grammaticality Judgements, Applied Linguistics, 19(2), 183-203

Deacon, T (1997) The Symbolic Species. The Co-Evolution of Language and the Human Brain. London: Allen Lane The Penguin Press

DFE (1995) English in the National Curriculum London: HMSO

DFE (1995) Geography in the National Curriculum London: HMSO

DFE (1995) History in the National Curriculum London: HMSO

DfEE (1996) Circular 9/95. Grants for Education and training. London: Department for Education and Employment

DfEE (1998) The National Literacy Strategy. Framework for Teaching London: Department for Education and Employment

De Graaf, R (1997) The Experanto Experiment. Effects of Explicit Instruction on Second Language Acquisition, Studies in Second Language Acquisition 19(2), 249-276

DeKeyser, R M (1997) Beyond Explicit Rule Learning: Automatizing Second Language Morphosyntax, Studies in Second Language Acquisition 19(2), 195-221

Demetras, M J, Post, K N and Snow, C (1986) Feedback to First Learners: the Role of Repetitions and Clarification Questions, Journal of Child Language, 13(2), 275-292

Dewey, J (1958) Experience and Nature. New York: Dover Publications

Doughty, C (1991) Second Language Instruction does make a difference: evidence from an empirical study of SL relativization, Studies in Second Language Acquisition 13(4), 431-469

Dulay, H and Burt, M (1973) Should We Teach Children Syntax? Language Learning, 23, 245-258

Dulay, H and Burt, M (1974c) Natural Sequences in Child Second Language Acquisition, Language Learning, 24, 37-53

Dulay, H and Burt, M (1974d) A New Perspective on the Creative Construction Processes in Child Second Language Acquisition, Language Learning, 24, 253-278

Ellis, N (1997) The Epigenesis of Language: Acquisition as a Sequence Learning Problem, BAAL: Evolving Models of Language, 12, 41-57

Ellis, R (1990) Instructed Second Language Acquisition. Oxford: Blackwell

Ellis R (1994) The Study of Second Language Acquisition. Oxford: Oxford University Press

Ellman, J L (1990) Finding Structure in Time, Cognitive Science, 14(2), 179-211

Farrar, M J (1992) Negative Evidence and Grammatical Morpheme Acquisition, Developmental Psychology, 28(1), 90-98

Fletcher, P and B MacWhinney (eds) (1995) The Handbook of Child Language. Oxford: Blackwell

Fotos, S S (1993) Consciousness Raising and Noticing through Focus on Form: Grammar Task Performance versus Formal Instruction, Applied Linguistics 14, 385-407

Gallaway, C and Richards, B J (1994) Input and Interaction in Language Acquisition. Cambridge: Cambridge University Press

Gardner, H (1983) Frames of Mind. New York: Basic Books

Gardner, R (1998) Between Speaking and Listening: the Vocalisation of Understandings, Applied Linguistics 19(2), 204-224

Gold, E M (1967) Language Identification in the Limit, Information and Control, 10(5), 447-474)

Gopnik, A and Meltzoff, A N (1986) Relationships Between Semantic and Cognitive Development: the Specificity Hypothesis, Child Development, 57, 1040-1053

Greenfield, S (1997) The Human Brain. A Guided Tour. London: Weidenfeld and Nicolson

Greenbaum, S and Quirk, R (1990) A Student's Grammar of the English Language Harlow: Longman

Hadley, I L (1987) Understanding Cohesion – Some Practical Teaching Implications, Reading, 21(2), 106-114

Hakes, D T (1980) The Development of Metalinguistic Abilities in Children. Berlin: Springer-Verlag

Halliday, M A K (1975) Learning How to Mean. Explorations in the Development of Language. London: Edward Arnold

Halliday, M A K (1994) An Introduction to Functional Grammar. Second Edition. London: Arnold

Harley, B (1989) Functional Grammar in French Immersion: a Classroom Experiment Applied Linguistics 10, 331-359

Harper, G F, Maheady L and Mallette B (1994) The Power of Peer-Mediated Instruction: How and why it creates academic success for all students, in J. S. Thousand, R. A. Villa and A. I. Nevin (eds) Creativity and Collaborative Learning, 229-241. Baltimore: Paul H. Brookes Publishing Co

Haworth, A (1992) Towards a Collaborative Model of Learning English in Education, 26(3), 40-49

Hebb, D O, Lambert, W E and Tucker, G R (1971) Language, Thought and Experience, The Modern Language Journal, LV(4), 212-222

Hoff-Ginsberg, E (1990) Maternal Speech and the Child's Development of Syntax: a Further Look, Journal of Child Language, 17(1), 85-99

Honey, J (1997) Language is Power. The Story of Standard English and its Enemies. London: Faber and Faber

Hornby, P A (1971) Surface Structure and the Topic-Comment Distinction: A Developmental Study, Child Development, 42, 1975-1988

Howe, C J (1993) Language Learning. A Special Case for Developmental Psychology? Hove: Lawrence Erlbaum Associates

Karmiloff-Smith A (1985) Language and Cognitive Processes from a Developmental Perspective, Language and Cognitive Processes 1, 61-85

Krashen, S D (1985) The Input Hypothesis. Issues and Implications. London: Longman

Krashen S D (1987) Principles and Practice in Second language Acquisition. London: Prentice-Hall International

Kress G and Knapp G (1992) Genre in a Social Theory of Language, English in Education 26(2), 4-15

Labov, W (1972) Language in the Inner City. Studies in the Black English Vernacular. Philadelphia: University of Pennsylvania Press

Leech, G and Svartvik J (1975) A Communicative Grammar of English. Harlow: Longman

Lightbown, P M and Spada, N (1996) How Languages are Learned. Oxford: Oxford University Press

Logan, G (1992) Shapes of Reaction Time Distribution and Shapes of Learning Curves: a test of the Instance Theory of Automaticity, Journal of Experimental Psychology: Learning, Memory and Cognition, 18, 883-914

Lyster, R and Ranta, L (1997) Corrective Feedback and Learner Uptake: Negotiation of Form in Communicative Classrooms, Studies in Second Language Acquisition, 19(1), 37-66

MacWhinney, B (1997) Implicit and Explicit Processes. Commentary, Studies in Second Language Acquisition, 19(2), 277-281

Martohardjono, G and Flynn, S (1995) Is There an Age Factor for Universal Grammar? In D Singleton and Z Lengyel (eds) The Age Factor in Second Language Acquisition, Clevedon: Multilingual Matters

McNeill, D (1966) Developmental Psycholinguistics, in F Smith and G A Miller (eds) The Genesis of Language. A Psycholinguistics Approach. Cambridge, Massachusetts: The M I T Press

McNeill, D (1971) The Capacity for the Ontogenesis of Grammar, in D I Slobin, The Ontogenesis of Grammar, New York: Academic Press

McNeil, M (1994) Creating Powerful Partnerships through Partner Learning, in J. S. Thousand, R. A. Villa and A. I. Nevin (eds) Creativity and Collaborative Learning, 243-259. Baltimore: Paul H. Brookes Publishing Co

MacWhinney, B (1997) Implicit and Explicit Processes. Commentary. Studies in Second Language Acquisition, 19(2), 277-281

Mahey, M (1978) The Great Piratical Rumbustification and The Librarian and the Robbers. Harmondsworth: Puffin Books

Murray, D E (1992) Collaborative Writing as a Literacy Event: Implications for ESL Instruction, in D Nunan (ed) Collaborative Language Learning And Teaching, 100-117. Cambridge: Cambridge University Press

Murray, F B (1994) Why Understanding the Theoretical Basis of Cooperative Learning Enhances Teaching Success in J. S. Thousand, R. A. Villa and A. I. Nevin (eds) Creativity and Collaborative Learning 3-11. Baltimore: Paul H. Brookes Publishing Co

Naigles, L R and Hoff-Ginsberg, E (1998) Why Are Some Verbs Learned Before Other Verbs? Effects of Input Frequency and Structure on Children's Early Verb Use, Journal of Child Language, 25, 95-120

Nelson, K E (1977) Facilitating Children's Syntax Acquisition, Developmental Psychology, 13(2), 101-107

Nelson, K E, Carskaddon, G and Bonvillian, J D (1973) Syntax Acquisition: Impact of Experimental Variation in Adult Verbal Interaction with the Child. Child Development, 44(4), 497-504

Nesdale, A R , Herriman, M L and Turner, W E (1984) Phonological Awareness in Children. In W E Tunmer, C Pratt and M L Herriman (eds) Metalinguistic Awareness in Children: Theory, Research, and Implications,105-205. Berlin: Springer-Verlag

Ochs, E and Schieffelin, B (1995) 'The Impact of Language Socialization on Grammatical Development' in P. Fletcher and B. MacWhinney (eds) The Handbook of Child Language, 73-94. Oxford: Blackwell

O'Donnel, R C, Griffin, W J and Norris, R (1967) Syntax of Kindergarten and Elementary School Children: A Transformational Analysis Research Report No 8: National Council of Teachers of English USA

Oliver, R (1995) Negative Feedback in Child NS-NNS Conversation, Studies in Second Language Acquisition, 17(4), 459-481

Owen, D (1996) Do Teachers modify their speech according to the proficiency of their students? English Language Teacher. Education and Development, 2(1), 31-51

Pagett, L (1992) Café' Conversation: 'Talk about Talk' in the Primary School – an Opportunity to Refine Children's Knowledge of Register and Genre in Diverse social Settings, English in Education 26(2), 62-67

Perera, K (1984) Children's Writing and Reading: Analysing Classroom Language. Oxford: Basil Blackwell in association with Andre Deutsch

Piaget, J (1959) The Language and Thought of the Child. London: Routledge

Plunkett, K (1995) 'Connectionist Approaches to Language Acquisition' in P. Fletcher and B. MacWhinney (eds) The Handbook of Child Language, 36-72. Oxford: Blackwell

Pratt, C and Grieve, R (1984) Metalinguistic Awareness and Cognitive Development, in W E Tunmer, C Pratt and M L Herriman (eds) Metalinguistic Awareness in Children: theory, research and implications, 128-143. Berlin: Springer-Verlag

Pratt, C and Nesdale, A R (1984) Pragmatic Awareness in Children. In W E Tunmer, C Pratt and M L Herriman (eds) Metalinguistic Awareness in Children: Theory, Research, and Implications,105-205. Berlin: Springer-Verlag

Pratt, C, Tunmer, W E and Bowey, J A (1984) Children's Capacity to Correct Grammatical Violations in Sentences, Journal of Child Language 11, 129-141

Robinson, P (1997) Generalizability and Automaticity of Second Language Learning under Implicit, Incidental, Enhanced and Instructed Conditions Studies, Second Language Acquisition 19(2), 223-247

Roth, F P (1984) Accelerating Language Learning in Young Children, Journal of Child Language, 11, 89-107

Sampson, G (1997) Educating Eve. The 'Language Instinct Debate'. London: Cassell

Saxton, M, Kulcsar, B, Marshall, G and Rupra, M (1988) Long-term Effects of Corrective Input: an Experimental Approach, Journal of Child Language, 25(3), 701-721

Scott, D, Hurry, J, Hey, V and Smith, M (1998) Developing Literacy in Inner-city Schools, English in Education 32(3), 27-33

Sebeok. T A (1994) An Introduction to Semiotics. London: Pinter Publishers

Shi, R, Morgan, J L and Allopenna, P (1998) Phonological and Acoustic bases for Earliest Grammatical Assignments: a Cross-Linguistic Perspective, Journal of Child Language, 25, 169-201

Singleton, D and Lengyel, Z (1995) (eds) The Age Factor in Second Language Acquisition. Clevedon: Multilingual Matters

Spada, N and Lightbown, P M (1993) Instruction and the Development of Questions in L2 Classrooms, Studies in Second Language Acquisition 15(2), 205-224

Staats, A W (1971) Linguistic Mentalistic Theory Versus an Explanatory S-R Learning Theory of Language Development. In D I Slobin (ed) The Ontogenesis of Grammar, New York: Academic Press

Stephens, J (1985) The Island. London: ILEA

Titone, R (1993) A Crucial Psycholinguistic Prerequisite to Reading: children's metalinguistic awareness, Scientia Paedagogica Experimentalis xxx(I), 81-96

Tunmer, W E and Grieve, R (1984) Syntactic Awareness in Children. In W E Tunmer, C Pratt and M L Herriman (eds) Metalinguistic Awareness in Children: Theory, Research, and Implications, 92-104. Berlin: Springer-Verlag

Udvari-Solner, A (1994) A Decision-Making Model for Curricular Adaptations in Cooperative Groups in J. S. Thousand, R. A. Villa and A. I. Nevin (eds) Creativity and Collaborative Learning 59-77. Baltimore: Paul H. Brookes Publishing Co

Valente, V G (1982) Dizionario Manfredoniano con Grammatica, Roma: Manzella Edizioni Scientifiche e Letterarie

Vygotsky, L (1934) Thought and Language. Translated and edited 1989 by A Kozulin. Cambridge, Massachusetts: The M I T Press

VanPatten, B and Cadierno, T (1993) Explicit Instruction and Input Processing Studies in Second Language Acquisition 15(2), 225-243

Wishart, E (1987) Textual Cohesion and Effective Reading: a Teaching Strategy Reading 21(1), 30-42

Yang, L R and Givon, T (1997) Benefits and Drawbacks of Controlled Laboratory Studies of Second Language Acquisition: The Keck Second Language Learning Project Studies in Second Language Acquisition 19(2), 173-193